T0293608

ROUTLEDGE LIBRARY EDITIONS:
MANAGEMENT

Volume 38

BOSSES IN BRITISH BUSINESS

BOSSES IN BRITISH BUSINESS

Managers and management from the Industrial Revolution to the present day

F. R. JERVIS

LONDON AND NEW YORK

First published in 1974 by Routledge & Kegan Paul Ltd

This edition first published in 2018
by Routledge
2 Park Square, Milton Park, Abingdon, Oxon OX14 4RN

and by Routledge
711 Third Avenue, New York, NY 10017

Routledge is an imprint of the Taylor & Francis Group, an informa business

British Library Cataloguing in Publication Data
A catalogue record for this book is available from the British Library

ISBN: 978-1-138-55938-7 (Set)
ISBN: 978-1-351-05538-3 (Set) (ebk)
ISBN: 978-0-8153-7012-3 (Volume 38) (hbk)
ISBN: 978-1-351-25068-9 (Volume 38) (ebk)

Publisher's Note
The publisher has gone to great lengths to ensure the quality of this reprint but points out that some imperfections in the original copies may be apparent.

Disclaimer
The publisher has made every effort to trace copyright holders and would welcome correspondence from those they have been unable to trace.

Bosses in British Business

Managers and management from the Industrial Revolution to the present day

F. R. Jervis

Routledge & Kegan Paul
London and Boston

First published in 1974
by Routledge & Kegan Paul Ltd
Broadway House, 68–74 Carter Lane,
London EC4 5EL and
9 Park Street,
Boston, Mass. 02108, U.S.A.
Printed in Great Britain by
Butler & Tanner Ltd, Frome and London
and set in Linotype Baskerville

ISBN 0 7100 7803 X
Library of Congress Catalog Card No. 73-91032

Contents

Preface

The failure of Upper Clyde Shipbuilders and of Rolls-Royce in recent times came as a severe shock to many people. In the one case there was the amalgamation of old and famous shipyards in an area which stood for shipbuilding excellence getting into deep trouble, while at the same time other yards further down the river were still profitable. In the other case a firm whose name was magic in the supply of luxury motor cars had to call in the Receiver, owing to a particularly unprofitable contract on aero engines, which had nothing to do with motor cars. The business is split up, Rolls-Royce Motors is hived off to raise the money to pay off the creditors and a separate company continues with the aero engine business.

But antiquity, respectability and reputation are no defence in a commercial world. Businesses fall as well as rise. As the ancients knew, the wheel of fortune is constantly turning and men are sometimes at the top and sometimes at the bottom. There is always great uncertainty. The economist would explain this by changes in conditions, changes in supply, in costs, and above all in demand for the product. But economic forces do not operate in a vacuum. Much, too, depends on the people, on the management of the firms – on the bosses. These bosses are broadly of two kinds. There is the owner entrepreneur or business founder, and the salaried manager who is so evident in the larger public companies and public boards. This book is concerned with the people, and examines some of the more interesting managers and business leaders and their reactions to the many problems of business management. By examining the reasons for success or failure pitfalls may be avoided and efficiency improved.

F. R. J.

The directors of such companies, however, being the managers rather of other people's money than of their own, it cannot well be expected that they should watch over it with the same anxious vigilance with which the partners in a private copartnery frequently watch over their own. . . . Negligence and profusion, therefore, must always prevail, more or less, in the management of the affairs of such a company.

Adam Smith, *The Wealth of Nations,* 1776

One

The founding fathers – rags to riches

> I believe that the principal reason why some firms survive, prosper and expand, while others dwindle, perish or sell out must be sought in the personalities of the men who manage them.
>
> C. Wilson, *The History of Unilever*, p. 44

Today we have the curious paradox that never before has there been such an interest in business matters and businessmen, yet this is coupled with a common disparagement of their activities. The attack on businessmen is often political but sometimes based on ignorance of the nature of the problems and the motivations facing them. Some of the severest criticisms of the actions of businessmen, such as the unacceptable face of capitalism, which arose from the dispute in the boardroom of Lonrho, have been made by politicians who are responsible for the law which regulates the actions of joint-stock companies. People who should have known better expressed surprise at certain events as though they were quite new, when they were common to many companies. The temptation to jump on the band-wagon of criticism proved irresistible. At Lonrho there was a deep division of opinion between the director who was the main driving force and the rest of the board – a very common phenomenon although it is often concealed from outsiders. The fact that some payments are made in foreign currencies in companies with world-wide operations is quite usual. But the so-called tax havens are a matter between the individual recipient and his tax inspector, and the rules for treatment of this money are laid down in the many Finance Acts. The fact that directors obtain benefits from their companies is as old as joint-stock companies. The fact that certain matters are concealed has excited company-law reformers ever since joint-stock-company registration was started in 1844. Company directors act within the framework of the current company law, or suffer the consequences.

The law on the subject is being revised constantly and brought up to date to deal with changing circumstances. This is not our concern here. But one effect of legal changes has been to increase the flow of information available. Before 1928 it was not even necessary for a public company to publish its accounts. Later the secretive got round the publication provisions by forming a holding company to own the private operating company so that the only assets that were disclosed were the shares and investments in subsidiary companies, without giving any indication of the real assets. After 1948 companies had to publish consolidated accounts bringing in all assets and liabilities. Future reforms will probably require greater disclosure of the different assets and operations of the company. Many companies today go far beyond the minimum requirements of the law. There is the contrast between the single-page company report of prewar days with the lavishly illustrated report freely distributed now. Many newspapers have business sections which deal with current problems and are not confined to share tips.

Yet in spite of greater publication and discussion there is often surprising ignorance of certain elementary commercial matters. One finds certain fallacies and errors being constantly repeated. They occur with distressing frequency in examination papers. There are politicians who use the expression 'private company' when they mean private industry. The people who make the law ought to be aware of the important distinction between the public and the private company. Companies are often referred to as being bodies owned by a few rich shareholders. It never was entirely true, the railway companies, for one example, were trustee stocks and attracted a lot of small investors. It is much less true now with the greater diffusion of ownership encouraged by company management and newspaper education in the mysteries of stocks and shares.

This is one of the dilemmas of working in this field. Matters which are plain common sense to those who have studied the subject prove to be very uncommon. The conventional wisdom of even educated and knowledgeable people is all too often economic fallacies. So the readers who find some statement a mere truism must bear with the author. They know it is a truism but there are many others who do not. Let them switch on the news and listen to the next proposal to nationalise *private* companies!

The purpose of this book is to examine one aspect of business operation. Broadly speaking we can draw a distinction between the entrepreneur, the founder and owner-manager of a business who risks his own money in the venture, and the manager of such a business who is dependent on his salary and who probably has a minimum investment. It is an investigation into the contrasts between the entrepreneur and the salaried manager but that is too cumbersome a title so the word boss is used to cover both operators. It is not a new problem, as Adam Smith recognised in his rather disparaging remarks about the managers of other people's money, but it is a problem which is of greater importance than in his day. The reason is the change in the balance of business structure.

Two hundred years ago, at the time of the Industrial Revolution, the typical business unit was the sole trader or the partnership. Companies were rare and generally confined to those with a royal charter such as the Bank of England and the East India Company, or those created by Act of Parliament such as canal, gas and railway companies. Today the joint-stock company is the typical business unit, with thousands of shareholders, and professional managers replacing the founders.

This change in business structure, although real, must not be exaggerated. It must be remembered that nearly all our very large businesses are of comparatively recent origin, certainly at their present size. Machine methods of production and concentrations of capital have aided the development of the large firm. The motor car industry is often given as an example of large-scale production cutting out the small firm, yet the large factories are assembly plants. The production line assembles thousands of different parts into one vehicle. These are made by thousands of different suppliers, some very large firms and yet many of them small, one-man engineering firms in back streets. In the building and construction industry, to take another example, firms range in size from the large contractor who will put up a tower block, down to the local builder who will erect a few houses, and ending with the brass plate plumber who will fit a new washer on a tap. Each has his place, and each is of the appropriate size for the type of work undertaken.

Thus the way is still open for a man of ability to start in a small way and gradually expand his business until it competes with the giants. The postwar world is full of examples. Some years ago the author was interviewing a large number of heads of moderate-sized family businesses. What was particularly striking was not only the difference between them and the employee-manager, but the similarity between them and their attitudes and what was known of some of the famous historical figures. Such people would not make good executives in a modern corporation but would be at home with William Morris or Boulton and Watt and Josiah Wedgwood. The similarities are to be found not with people in the same historical period but with people in the same stage of business development.

The pioneers

Boulton and Watt[1] is the classic partnership between the clever, poor and shy inventor with the equally clever, rich, urbane and efficient manufacturer; Boulton was 'the first manufacturer of England' and according to Boswell 'an iron chieftain, a father to his tribe'. Watt's difficulties in applying his improvement to the Newcomen engine were partly financial and partly technical. He was skilled in the manufacture of small items but the ability to make the larger cylinders to the required accuracy was generally lacking in England. Watt had entered into a partnership with Roebuck at the Carron Ironworks to provide steam power for pumping but the works failed, partly owing to Roebuck's finances and also – what was to become a familiar story in modern technology – because the new engine proved unsatisfactory. Boulton was one of Roebuck's creditors and in satisfaction of the debt took over the latter's share in the steam engine patent. This was a great act of faith in Watt as none of the other creditors put the value at a farthing. The partnership of Boulton and Watt was set up in 1775 for the design and manufacture of steam engines. Watt was a partner in this business only, while Boulton had other partnerships, successful and unsuccessful, in his other activities.

It was Boulton's capital, his scientific interest in this and other matters, and the quality of the workmen he had trained in the Soho foundry, which eventually made the modern steam engine. Watt could concentrate on 'research and development' without financial and administrative worries.

Abraham Darby, senior, succeeded in smelting iron ore with coke instead of charcoal. This solved the problem of the eighteenth-century fuel crisis. The firm was responsible for many improvements in the iron trade, but our main interest here in this Quaker business was in the series of partnerships and the influx of managerial ability which enabled the firm to survive (see below, chapter 2). It is now part of Allied Ironfounders.

Whether Richard Arkwright was the true inventor of the patents he took out or whether he used the ideas of others is one of the disputed facts of history. But what is undisputed is that he made the ideas work and he was the 'inventor' of the modern factory system. More than technical ability in the spinning process was required. John Wyatt for example, one of the early inventors,[2]

> did not succeed. . . . He was of a gentle and passive spirit, little qualified to cope with the hardships of a new manufacturing enterprise. It required in fact a man of a Napoleonic nerve and ambition to subdue the refractory tempers of workpeople accustomed to irregular paroxysms of diligence, and to urge on his multifarious and intricate constructions in the face of passion, prejudice and envy.

First, Arkwright set up a series of factories, based originally on water and then on steam power, going up the Derwent valley into Lancashire and Scotland. He provided the technical expertise and the managerial ability. He was adept at forming the right type of partnerships; with merchants such as the Strutts of Belper who provided the outlets, with landowners who provided the land and water courses, and with bankers who provided finance. In all these partnerships, with different people, he was always the guiding hand.

W le the new rich, nonconformist, radical factory owners were much criticised by the old rich, Church of England, Tory landowners who seldom saw a factory, or even the condition of their agricultural employees in winter, it is generally true that the poorest conditions of work existed in the least successful firms, and that many of the successful owners were considerate employers. They were influential in promoting the Factory Acts to bring the standard of the poorer managed factories up to that of the best; with the result that children were better protected in cotton factories than in other occupations – including agriculture and domestic service; wages were much higher, as John Bright the Quaker cotton spinner pointed out to Lord Ashley the 'establishment' landowner in one of their periodic disputes. Many of them were pioneers in providing education for their young employees.

Robert Owen is of course well known for his factory management, largely because he acquired a considerable reputation in other fields, for example early trade unions, co-operative societies and socialist communities, most of which failed. But he acquired with other partners the New Lanark Mills which had been founded by Arkwright and David Dale, and he there carried on the humane management instituted by Dale. His modern admirers would certainly not approve his technique of the 'Silent Monitor' which showed a different colour against each workman according to the quality of the work. It would cause an immediate strike!

The new factories provided a training ground for managers. Many of the owners were merchants or investors who took no direct part in the management of the factory, such as Drinkwater who gave Owen his first important post, and much was left to paid managers. Many were inefficient or dishonest but others used the opportunity of adding commercial knowledge to their technical skill and left to found their own businesses. They became the second generation of factory owners.

Many of the mills exist to this day although they are now part of larger groupings, such as Coats and English Sewing Cotton. Some used water power right into the twentieth century.

Machine tools

The Industrial Revolution depended on the manufacture of accurate machinery and on the industry to make this machinery. One of the curious features of this period is the great importance of a number of small craftsmen, often self-educated, who combined technical excellence with business ability, and provided an excellent training ground for others. There was an intimate interconnection between all these businesses. Many of the highly skilled engineers were prepared to branch out on their own and were not content to remain as managers of other people's works.

Joseph Bramah set up in London on his own and in 1778 invented the water closet. Later he developed the beer pump and the hydraulic press among other inventions. When he invented an improved lock there were not the skilled workmen to make it. (Compare this with Watt's steam engine.) The solution was to produce a set of machine tools that would guide the workman. He was introduced to Henry Maudsley, an eighteen-year-old tradesman at Woolwich Arsenal, who devised the necessary machinery. Maudsley worked for Bramah from 1789 to 1797 and became works manager. The normal expectation would have been a partnership but when this was not forthcoming Maudsley set up on his own. Later he took a partner, Joshua Field, a draughtsman who had worked in Portsmouth Dockyard, and the firm of Maudsley and Field was set up in 1805. It made machinery, perfected the slide rest for the lathe and developed the screw cutting lathe so that nuts and bolts were interchangeable. 'The vigilant, the critical, and yet withall the generous eye of the master being over all his workmen, it will be readily understood how Maudsley's works came to be regarded as a first-class school for mechanical engineers.'[3]

Joseph Clement taught himself and became a first-class workman. He came to London where he got employment with a man 'the height of whose ambition was to be an alderman', and like most corporation celebrities 'he held a low rank in his own business'.[4] So Clement left and went to Bramah and was put in charge of the tools in the shop, with a five-year contract. On Bramah's death, his sons returned from college and found Clement the ruling mind, so Clement left and became the chief draughtsman for Maudsley and Field. He accumulated about £500 and set up in business on his own account. He developed the planer and the lathe still further and became a regular manufacturer of taps and dies. Joseph Whitworth started work with Maudsley and then went to Clement before setting up on his own. He is the founder of the standardised Whitworth thread.

James Nasmyth, the inventor of the steam hammer, after serving as a personal assistant to Maudsley set up on his own in Manchester in 1834. There was plenty of work with the growth of the market in textile machinery and general engineering and Nasmyth followed the normal business practice of the partnership to increase his capital. He was alive to the possibilities of standard production in advance of orders. He sent out printed catalogues describing the machines available for sale. This meant a planned factory layout to mass produce the machines. The various workshops were all in a line, and so placed that the work proceeded from one operation to the other in its logical order. A railroad carried heavy materials through the works. There was a proper organisation of departmental functions and within three years the firm employed about 300 men. He made a fortune in twenty years.[5]

Josiah Wedgwood

It is well known that Josiah Wedgwood prospered because the conditions were right for him: the extension of tea drinking created the market; canal building brought raw materials and distributed the finished product, and his insistence on good workmanship and his up-to-date factory organisation lowered costs. But this does not tell the whole story and show where he differed from his rivals.[6]

His period was one of great technical advance and even where he led others could easily follow. His inventions of green glaze, cream ware, and jasper were soon copied and the large number of antiques which crowd the salesrooms today are evidence of the many other firms that produced excellent quality articles. His leadership in any of his new processes could not last for long. Others could follow the principle of division of labour, as laid down in theory by Adam Smith and as put into practice by well-known manufacturers such as Arkwright and Boulton and Watt. Wedgwood's search for perfection was costly and there were many technical failures; 10,000 pieces of jasper were made before he achieved perfection. His design costs were increased by the commissions given to well-known artists, and he paid relatively high wages. All this more than cancelled his low costs of production. He did not undersell his rivals; he beat them by charging often double and treble their prices. His business was based on high quality and fashionable appeal. He charged what the nobility would pay and he realised the simple truth that the high price in itself was part of the esteem in which his goods were held.

His belief was that 'fashion was superior to merit in many respects' and he sought sponsors among the monarchy, the nobility and the art connoisseurs; he became the Queen's Potter – a more rewarding title than the modern Queen's Award to Industry – and accepted individual orders if they had a good publicity value. His service for Catherine the Great consisted of 1,282 pieces and included a thousand original paintings. The fact that many of these paintings were of the stately homes excited the interest of their owners in the service, and drew them to his showrooms to see 'their piece'. He cultivated his clients by asking their advice and giving them advance notice of new designs; his aristocratic friends praised his ware, they advertised it, they bought it, and they took their friends to buy it. The lead of the aristocracy was followed by the rest of the community who could not afford to be unfashionable. It is a method of trading which is followed today by those who cultivate the endorsement of their products by the new aristocracy – film and television stars and prominent sportsmen.

He opened a showroom in London and this became one of the most fashionable meeting places. His example was followed by Boulton and Fothergill, Spode and Minton. He opened branch showrooms at Bath, pursuing his customers even on holiday, and at Liverpool and Dublin. Other business innovations were the provision of a pattern book in his showrooms, and the first recorded example of a satisfaction or money back guarantee – claimed by an American store as a 'first' nearly a hundred years afterwards – the provision of catalogues in foreign languages, and foreign clerks to answer letters in the native tongue.

Although Wedgwood is renowned for his technical excellence, his factory organisation and his inventive genius, his really distinguishing feature as compared with many who share some of these qualities is that he realised that in business it is the customer and the market which is the justification and the objective.

Railways

Waggons drawn on iron rails had been a feature of the Coalbrookdale works and the north-east collieries for many years, as part of their internal transport; the modern railway for the public conveyance of goods and passengers, built up into a comprehensive system, stemmed from the marriage of engineering ability in coal mining with the business foresight of Quaker businessmen.

When, after long discussion, the businessmen in Darlington finally decided on a railway instead of a canal for the carriage of coal from Darlington to Stockton, an Act of Parliament was obtained for a line worked by horses for merchandise only. But George Stephenson, a colliery engine-wright, persuaded Edward Pease and his associates to see what his locomotive could do. They were impressed and the Act was amended to allow for steam transport and the carriage of passengers. The well-known success of the 'Quaker line' was followed by others. In nearly every case the impetus came from local businessmen, many of them Quakers, who put their own money into the venture in order to improve transport facilities in their area, and had no support from the financial market or the government. The latter certainly did not believe in the idea of the technological revolution and was often grudging in approving new companies. As the railways grew in size they presented new administrative problems unknown to the businesses of that time. The only comparable large undertakings were armies, and army officers figured among the early managers. So, railways developed with a sense of discipline that facilitated their complicated operations. Different lines were consolidated into unified systems by such people as George Hudson, 'the railway king', who subsequently fell from grace but left his mark on the railway system.

The railway 'projectors' being merchants, landowners, bankers and industrialists obviously knew nothing about the new art of railway construction or operation, and had to rely on hiring, and judging, outside experts. The profession of the consulting engineer had developed with the canals a generation before, but the railways created the great opportunities. Although George Stephenson could not read or write at the age of eighteen and was very weak on theoretical knowledge he had a remarkable shrewdness and a great intuition on mechanical matters. He also inspired confidence, and the solid Quaker businessmen supported him in all controversies as they formed a high opinion of his character. He invented the miner's safety lamp at the same time as Sir Humphry Davy. The latter thought it inconceivable that an illiterate man could succeed in an undertaking which had occupied his own scientific attention! Stephenson received £1,000 in subscriptions for his invention and in the north-east collieries it was generally preferred because it had been developed under actual working conditions, yet few textbooks give him the credit.

The problem of building long lengths of line was usually solved by employing an engineer-surveyor to plan out the construction and supervise the work. The actual construction was split into manageable proportions by the principle of subcontracting sections of the line, and by the employment of specialists. While the Irish navvies shovelled across Britain, the platelayers were 'Geordies' chosen by Stephenson. Many of the subcontractors were people in a very small way of business, clubbing together to build a few miles of railway, or doing the brickwork on bridges, etc. But some developed into large and important businesses, comparable with

Stephenson's and Brunel's. Thomas Brassey started with quoting for a small stretch of line and eventually built up an organisation that laid railways in nearly every country in the world. Besides his great reputation for business probity (when a bridge collapsed during construction he gave immediate orders that it was to be rebuilt at his own expense) he was a great inspirer of his workmen. It was his men that the Parisians came out to see building the Paris–Rouen railway and caused them to exclaim 'Mon Dieu, les Anglais, comme ils travaillent!' He must have been one of the few heads of a large business whose visits to the works were not viewed with fear of the consequences but were welcomed as coming from a guide and a friend.

To provide the locomotives, a company, Robert Stephenson and Co., was set up with the Peases and their associates and George Stephenson and his son Robert in Newcastle. A similar firm, the Vulcan Foundry, was later founded to build locomotives for the Liverpool and Manchester railway. One result of the use of the same firms of consulting engineers and the purchase of engines from the same firms was a standardisation of equipment. The colliery gauge of 4 ft 8½ in. became the standard gauge in Britain and in many parts of the world. Brunel's 7 ft gauge was not only based on his belief that it had technical advantages, which may have been true, but on his commercial view that if the west country were broad gauge it would keep out competition from other companies. Stephenson had a wider vision; he foresaw the linking up of the small lines into a unified system.

The shopkeepers

The increase in population and in wealth in the nineteenth century caused fundamental changes in the economy. As larger markets developed, there were opportunities of new commercial undertakings.

Old towns such as London, Bristol and Norwich had developed adequate markets and shops; country districts relied on markets and on the annual fairs for the supply of 'consumer durables'; it was in the new industrial towns that a gap in facilities existed to be filled. Various attempts at voluntary co-operation in shopkeeping had been tried but these usually failed due to commercial inexperience. Goods were bought and sold near to cost price and then it was discovered that overhead costs had to be paid and such businesses often collapsed. The 'invention' came in 1844 in Rochdale. A group of people formed a Co-operative Society based on the principle that each member contributed to the capital cost of the enterprise. A shop was rented, and the more common articles of consumption were stocked. But instead of trying to compete with the local shops, the ruling price was accepted and a surplus on trading aimed at. (The word 'surplus' was preferred to the word 'profit'.) But instead of this surplus being distributed among the members in proportion to capital invested, as in joint-stock companies, it was paid out as a dividend in proportion to purchases. This principle of the 'deferred rebate' encouraged loyalty, and by leaving the dividend in the Society, it helped to develop working-class savings. Progress at first was slow, but eventually the shop opened full time and the range of goods was extended. But these 'entrepreneurs' were thinking beyond the limits of a small shop. They were thinking of building a new society by their own efforts. The ideas spread, often by imitation but more often by 'missionaries' from the successful Societies addressing meetings in other towns and getting Societies established.

Although each Co-operative Society is governed by the same rules and is actuated by the same basic philosophy, each is a separate business in the same way that different joint-stock companies are separate businesses registered under the Companies Acts – a simple fact which was unknown to the BBC when it suggested that because one or two small Co-operative Societies were in some difficulties, the whole movement was implicated; and a subsequent amending programme only served to make confusion worse confounded.

It was this sort of enterprise, coming from unexpected sources, which was to be found also in the rise of trade unions, friendly societies and mechanics' institutes, that inspired Samuel Smiles to write his book *Self Help*, showing that the 'ordinary working man' had the ability to improve his lot without relying on others.

The co-operative principle was imitated with the foundation of the Civil Service Stores, originally for post office workers. It was registered under the Industrial and Provident Society Acts in 1866, but in 1927 transferred to the company form. The Army and Navy Stores was registered as a company in 1871 but the business was based on an earlier history.

The department store

The successful shopkeeper who wishes to expand comes up against the 'distance limit'. No matter how great his reputation there is a limit beyond which his customers will not travel. The limit varies with the type of trade. While the 'little shop around the corner' for daily necessities attracts people from a very restricted area, a leading shop catering for large irregular purchases such as fashion clothing can attract people for the annual shopping expedition from all over the country, and even in some cases from abroad as well.

The problem of expansion can generally be solved in either of two ways: go after the customers by opening branch shops, or sell more to existing customers by stocking fresh lines. The department store, as its name implies, follows the latter course. It was the new prosperous middle-class market which provided the incentive.

The beginning of the modern department store is usually attributed to Aristide Boucicault who founded the Bon Marché in Paris in 1852 on the principle of a small mark-up on the cost of goods, a quick turnover of stock, and the clear marking of prices. (Many present-day British department stores were founded before this, but the businesses were not operated on these trading principles. They were ordinary shops.) His success was rapidly followed by the foundation of others, sometimes by former employees, such as the Louvre and the Printemps. With one notable exception, Selfridges, department stores in Britain were not consciously established; they just grew by force of circumstances.

William Whiteley had a thorough knowledge of the technique of his trade. He served an apprenticeship with the largest drapers in Wakefield in 1848, and at the end of his time came to London in 1855 with £10. He gained further experience with some of the most important wholesalers and became an expert on materials. He also saved £700, which proved his high earning capacity. In 1863 he opened a shop in Westbourne Grove with a staff of two girls and an errand boy. It was an instant success. Unlike many of the shops of the period, the customers were never pestered to buy, the goods were displayed to the best advantage, prices were marked in plain figures, and all goods were sold at a reasonable profit.

Within a year he had twelve assistants, a cashier and two errand boys. He had started by selling ribbons (his speciality), lace trimmings and fancy goods, and he added silks, linens, mantles, draperies and dresses, millinery, haberdashery, jewellery and furs. In 1867, when his sales were £43,000 a year, he took a lease of a second shop, and then another and another. In 1868 he undertook dressmaking, 1869 men's outfitting, 1870 costumes, 1871 tailoring, boots and hats, and in 1872 furnishing and drapery.

After 1872 he went far beyond his original scope. He became 'The Universal Provider'.[7] Often the impetus came from his customers who asked him to add fresh lines. He set up a house agency, provided refreshment rooms and cleaning and dyeing services. He occupied ten shops and employed over 600 people on the premises and 1,000 out of doors. He developed the 'departmental' system of management by engaging an experienced buyer to manage each new department and the buyer was responsible for engaging his own staff. In department store organisation the head of the selling department is known as the 'buyer' who is responsible for obtaining the right goods for the shop; the assistant buyer is normally responsible for the organisation of the selling trade. In this way the department is operated by a specialist in the trade, that is in fashion goods or furniture, and not by a salesman who sells anything. The store is a collection of different specialities under one roof operating under a common policy.

The large profits were reinvested in the business. Additional capital was raised from his customers by opening a banking department and paying 5 per cent interest on deposits. Customers could draw on their balances to settle accounts. Other stores, such as Harrods and Lewis's, have used the same technique. By 1876 the profit reached a peak that was not exceeded for ten years. The competition was beginning to intensify. There was a fresh burst of activity in 1886 and new departments were opened, including a hire department which would do anything; it made him famous when he provided an elephant for a customer (not from stock) and he is reputed to have supplied a second-hand coffin! He even entertained the Zulu chief Cetewayo on behalf of a harassed Colonial Office.

The dark side to this business success was his treatment of staff. There was a contrast between the urbane shopkeeper, popular with his lady customers, and the employer of labour.[8]

> The feature of life at Whiteley's which excited most discontent and criticism was the severe discipline. Many of the employees

> testified to the contrast between the bland and fatherly demeanour of the Universal Provider when first engaging a newcomer and the harsh and relentless fashion in which he would punish mistakes or dismiss offenders.

He instituted a system of fines which went straight into his own pocket, and the large number of legal prosecutions against employees proved that the store was not 'a happy ship'.

The business was beset by a series of fires which were unaccounted for, and which caused losses and necessitated rebuilding, and Whiteley ran into considerable debt to contractors and customers. Costs were rising, and as early as 1888 it began to be remarked that the Universal Provider's prices were no longer the lowest in the market and he was being undercut by his rivals. The store reached the limit of expansion with about 6,000 employees. The business was floated as a public company in 1889 but none of the shares was offered to the public and his customers were disappointed at not being able to participate in the business except by taking up debentures. Harrods did not make the same mistake but gave preference to local people, thus developing customer loyalty.

Whiteley was murdered in his office in 1907 not by an employee, which might have been understandable, but by an illegitimate son. So there was another side to his character not known to his admiring customers.

Most department stores developed from the drapery trade where it is easy to add fresh lines as the business expands. Harrods was the exception. Charles Harrod inherited from his father a small 'carriage trade' provision business, which he built up by a combination of high quality goods, business reputation and personal charm. But he could not delegate and even served in the shop when it was large enough to need a hundred employees. His friends said of him that if he did not learn to keep his coat on he would ruin the business. He also went public in 1889 and retired from the business. But as there was no adequate management the business went down and Harrod had to come back from retirement to pull the business together. The company got as general manager Richard Burbidge, who had had similar experience with the Army and Navy Stores and Whiteley and this proved to be its salvation. The business was managed by three generations of Burbidge until it was taken over by the House of Fraser. It is firmly entrenched at the 'quality end' of the trade, but in all justice it should be called Burbidges and not Harrods. It never had the ups and downs of Whiteleys, or its unenviable reputation.

Albert Gamage when shopping in Holborn was told that there was a good opportunity for a men's shop in the neighbourhood. He opened a hosiery shop and extended a mainly men's wear trade by good quality, low prices, large-scale advertising and special mail order goods. Located near the city it did not follow the normal practice of catering for women but specialised in male customers. The virtues of specialisation in one trade which could be done well were shown when the company tried to extend.

In 1928, when he had been succeeded by his son, the company formed a new company, Gamages West End, and opened a store in Oxford Street, where it was in competition with the well-established shops doing a different type of trade. The store was opened in September 1930 and closed by the Receiver in April 1931. There had been a lack of capital from the start, the new building had proved more costly to erect than had been anticipated, and the construction took longer – a familiar story which is repeated to the present day in a variety of enterprises. The parent company lost some of its own turnover to the new store, and in addition to the failure of the subsidiary and the loss to the investors, the parent company had to reduce its capital to cover the losses.

A different form of exploiting the market was that of Lewis's. Most of the successful big stores were based on the main shopping areas of London. The provincial areas were developing with the growth of large commercial centres in Manchester, Liverpool and Birmingham. Lewis's realised that a shop which was catering successfully for the wives of the rising middle class in one town could do the same in another. It therefore followed the model of founding almost identical stores where wives had money to spend and leisure to shop. As the markets were similar, a little behind the more fashionable West End trade, it was possible to use the principle of bulk buying to reduce costs.

H. G. Selfridge had had a very successful career in America with Marshall Field and like Whiteley he was an excellent salesman. He had a poor opinion of British businessmen and thought that by the introduction of American selling methods he could 'clean up' the London market. With his own capital and some financial support he opened Selfridges in Oxford Street in 1908 as a fully fledged department store. All the established firms had grown from small beginnings.

The business was an instant success in the trade in which it specialised. Selfridge was a superb salesman and showman. He probably tapped new markets in London rather than took trade from his competitors. Of all the London stores his was the best known outside London, and Selfridge's 'bargain basement' was the Mecca for the provincial housewife up to town for a shopping spree. But his methods were basically no different from those of similar stores catering for a different section of the market, and he had been induced by his associates to tone down his ideas of more aggressive American salesmanship as the British market would not stand for it. His entertainments of celebrities and election night parties became famous, and kept the name of the store before the general public. But the super salesman also made serious mistakes (see chapter 3).

The multiples

Other people expanded their trade by the use of the opposite principle. The circle of customers was increased by opening additional shops to sell the same goods. The principle here was to concentrate on a narrow range of goods in which the founder became a specialist. Expansion could be easy as little capital expenditure was necessary. Small shops could be rented, fitted with standardised equipment and appearance so that one shop tended to advertise another. As the range of goods was limited, centralised control was facilitated. The manager was a promoted salesman who did not have to have the talents and expertise of the buyer in a department store. He sold what the head office provided, banked the cash daily, and made simple returns to head office weekly. As there was little provided in the way of choice, credit or delivery, the emphasis was on price. The multiple in the High Street undercut the private firm round the corner or the large specialist offering a range of goods.

Practically every town of moderate size had its local grocery chain of anything from half a dozen to a hundred branches and in addition there were those such as the Home and Colonial, Maypole Dairy, Meadow Dairy and Liptons in the provision trade which had a national coverage. These four are amalgamated into Allied Suppliers which has a link with Unilever. Most of these, and similar firms, had a prosperous but un-noteworthy history until the interwar years. The difficulty with many of them has been to adapt to different market conditions since the war.

The invention of new machinery for boots and shoes gave rise to a large number of multiple firms, generally family businesses. Some started from manufacture and opened shops to sell their own output. This often led to difficulties later, as with Lennards and The Benefit Company when the factories were no longer producing the type of footwear required by the market: the rising standard of living resulted in a change from heavy boots to lighter shoes. Others started as shops and went back into manufacture; others, and the more successful, stuck to the specialised trade of retailing, buying their supplies from the many specialised manufacturers. Shops must carry a wide range of goods, men's, women's, children's, boots and shoes, slippers, etc., while manufacture generally takes place in separate factories, and even in separate parts of the country, which specialise in one item only. A number of these firms have disappeared into the maw of larger mergers, but the family-controlled public company, with 200–250 branches, still survives.

Similar moderate-sized family businesses are to be found in men's outfitting multiples, and like the footwear shops, have generally an uneventful history.

This could not be said for the Lipton business. Lipton set up as a provision merchant in Glasgow in 1876, where he soon acquired a good reputation for curing hams. In 1889 he entered the tea trade with a great flourish. His first purchase, of 20,000 chests of tea, was escorted through the streets of Glasgow by a pipe band to inform the citizens that 'Lipton's tea was coming'. Glasgow was not large enough and he moved his headquarters to London, and twenty-two years later when the business was converted into a public company it had expanded to include 242 branches, twelve Ceylon estates to grow his own tea, and factories to manufacture cocoa, chocolate, confectionery, jam, marmalade, preserves, biscuits and beef extract.

By 1919 there were nearly 500 branches and by 1921 over 550, when the business reached its peak. Dividends of 12½ per cent were paid for the years 1918 to 1923, 10 per cent in 1924 and nil in the next three years. The vast, diversified, backward integrated business was too complicated to manage, at least by the current management. The management was taken over by the Meadow Dairy Company and there was much writing down of overvalued assets. The business could not be controlled by one man whose interests lay elsewhere, and who found it easier to obtain a knighthood than to gain admission to the Royal Yacht Squadron. There are parallels with the career of Selfridge; both were innovating salesmen, both attracted influential friends and backers, both were pillars of society, both overexpanded, and both virtually ruined the businesses they had created.

Until the time of Montague Burton there was little between the expensive made-to-measure clothes of the rich and the poor-quality 'reach-me-downs' of the workman. In 1900 Burton borrowed £100 from a relative and opened a shop in Chesterfield. By 1907 he had developed a small chain of shops, and by 1952 had 700 shops and 10,500 employees by the simple idea of applying mass-production methods to a backward cottage industry, and by offering the working man bespoke tailoring of good-quality materials at low prices. He integrated production with the market, made cash sales instead of the usual long-term credit which prevailed in tailoring, and aimed at a quick turnover. Moreover, his employees in the numerous factories worked in bright conditions instead of the 'sweat shops' of the period.

A similar organisation, Price's Tailors, known in the interwar years as the Fifty Shilling Tailors, followed the same lines. It also looked to the market and its policy was to cater for the average wage earner, 'who cannot afford to pay, roughly, more than one week's wages for a suit of clothes'.

In the early eighteenth century it was the West of England clothiers who 'clothed the gentlemen of England' but in the twentieth it was the multiple specialists who clothed the bulk of the male population, at considerably less expense.

Montague Gluckstein on his travels round the country for his tobacco firm, Salmon and Gluckstein, noticed the difficulty of getting good light refreshments except in public houses, and saw that there was a market for an improved catering service. The partners started by offering catering at various exhibitions and registered the business as J. Lyons and Co. in 1887. Lyons was an associate and his name was used because of the disadvantage of associating catering with a tobacco firm. A number of small tea shops was set up and the business grew quickly. The tobacco business disappeared into the Imperial Tobacco Company amalgamation and the members of the families concentrated on the new venture. The company 'traded up' by establishing the Trocadero and a number of Corner Houses in London. These were similar to the magnificent palaces of the luxury super cinemas of the interwar years where the customers could bask in the illusion of a brighter world beyond the reach of their income.

Lyons claimed, with justification, that it had contributed to the social revolution by providing good tea shops, where a man could take a lady, instead of poor taverns and 'slap bangs' with slovenly waitresses. The ABC (Aerated Bread Company), which had been founded on a new method of making bread in 1862, has a similar claim. The story is that one of the manageresses 'obliged' her customers by making tea for them, and the idea spread to other branches. The Express Dairy Company was formed in 1880 after the cattle plague in the city reduced the supply of milk. It introduced a system of fast horse-drawn carts to bring in a supply of fresh milk from the country, and also developed tea shops.

The variety chain

The variety chain type of business was based on the principle of selling a variety of goods at a number of stores, within a definite price range, provided there was sufficient turnover to justify the trade. It started in America with the 'five and ten' (cents) as the basic price, and the founder of F. W. Woolworth failed four times before finding the successful formula. Subsidiary companies have been opened in many other countries. There was a rapid expansion in the interwar years, as with the general fall in prices new lines could be brought within the price range. During and after the war these businesses were faced with the dilemma of keeping to the self-imposed price limits or of trading up to higher price ranges. Now the 'five and ten' is a distant memory – like the fifty shilling suit or the penny post.

Marks and Spencer started as a market stall and then became a series of 'Penny Bazaars' where all goods were sold at a penny. In the interwar years the firm traded up to an upper limit of five shillings. Most prices took advantage of the old draper's custom of knocking a farthing off the price – i.e. 19*s.* 11¾*d.* where the customer got a farthing change or a packet of pins. In this case it was a full penny. Articles were priced at 4*s.* 11*d.*; 2*s.* 11*d.*, etc.

The main expansion, however, came from a thorough study of the market, within their definite price range. Instead of the company asking the common question, what price will we have to put on this article to make a profit? – the cost-plus mentality – it started from the other end. How many of these can be sold at 4*s.* 11*d.*? What different types and styles will sell in the largest quantities? Then the problem was to get the goods made to an exact specification, with long order runs, within this price limit. The policy was 'the greatest good for the greatest number'. Not all types or sizes would be stocked, but only those which had the largest turnover. For example, if analysis showed that in ladies' blouses 50 per cent of the demand would be for white, 10 per cent for blue, and 10 per cent for red, these colours only were stocked, with a rapid turnover. The customer who wanted something different in colour or style or size could go to the small specialist shop with its lower turnover and higher prices, or go to the department store.

The sensible, basic principle of concentrating on doing a limited thing supremely well, and of producing what the customer wants rather than trying to sell what is interesting to produce, or what the firm has always produced, is one which so many firms seem unable to grasp. Neither has Marks and Spencer fallen into the trap of thinking that it can manufacture a large variety of goods cheaper than the specialist producers.

Soap

A further improvement in the standard of living of the mass of the population came with the cheapening in the manufacture of soap and its increasing use by all classes. In the eighteenth century there were a number of localised, moderate-sized family businesses, such as R. S. Hudson, Joseph Watson, John Knight with its high quality 'Royal Primrose' and Pears, one of the first firms to develop advertising with its use of Millais's 'Bubbles'.

But the modern soap industry was made by a newcomer, William Lever. He entered his father's wholesale grocery business in 1867 at the age of sixteen. As an apprentice – apprenticeship was still the normal 'business education' – he received an excellent and thorough business training. He persuaded his father to let him travel for the firm, using the convincing argument that he was saving money by quitting the office as travellers were paid more than clerks. He had obvious ability, as his father took him into partnership at the age of twenty-one at a salary of £800 a year! He was self-educated and read widely. With his friends he set up book-reading circles, visited lectures and theatres, which was just permitted in his middle-class, respectable environment. According to Dr Charles Wilson[9] he had a healthy and catholic course of self-education, and many a university provides worse.

The market was expanding but Lever was not content to wait for it to develop. He advertised Irish butter in the Press and brought over large supplies. By 1884 the potentialities of the grocery business were exhausted and Lever looked round for something else. He decided that he could push soap through his retail outlets and had it made for him by a number of manufacturers. Then he registered the trade name 'Sunlight' and had the soap wrapped, with the name on the wrapper. As he was not satisfied with the quality of the soap bought he decided to go into manufacture. He took over an existing factory in 1885 but as this proved uneconomic his solution was to start from the beginning with a completely fresh site. In 1889 he established Port Sunlight where there was excellent water and rail transport and ample space for extension.

A private company was registered in 1890 and it went public in 1894, with a capital of £1½ million, half in 5 per cent preference shares. He eventually owned all the ordinary shares himself as he bought out his fellow directors with preference shares, as 'his colleagues were men of more modest and ordinary talents and their cautious hesitancy was a constant irritation to him'. The business extended as he advertised extensively for the growing working-class market. In the 1880s he was living modestly and ploughing back the remainder of his £50,000 a year income.

Even as a public company the business was still operated in an autocratic manner by Lever as a personal possession. The success had been so rapid that Lever extended into many other activities, some successful but many not so. As Dr Wilson points out, 'Lever's success was built on originality (Sunlight) and where he had nothing new to offer, in a market already overcrowded with competent and established competitors, not all his energy, optimism, and advertising skill could command success. Where he led, he conquered; where he followed, he fell.'

Other firms in the same trade were bought out; R. S. Hudson in

1908 to get into the soap powder business, Price's Patent Candle Company and John Knight after the war. He went into the allied trade of margarine (similar raw materials and the same retail outlets). An arrangement was made with the Maypole Dairy Company for the manufacture and distribution of margarine. A joint committee of the two companies met fortnightly. But two autocratic chiefs could not work together and Planter's margarine passed into Lever's control in 1915.

But there were failures, or at least a lack of success in many of the ventures which were often a result of the personal whim of the autocrat. After a holiday in the Hebrides he established MacFisheries, a chain of fishmongers to help the sturdy fishermen he admired on his holiday; chocolate and confectionery businesses were sold in 1932; the integration backwards to plantations, the Niger Company and the United Africa Company, was unsuccessful when the fall in raw material prices meant that supplies could be obtained more cheaply from outside sources; even his share of the soap market had been gradually falling since the 1920s, and the small man had more than held his own. When he died in 1925, Lord Leverhulme left a ramshackle business that was virtually unmanageable (see below, chapter 3).

William Morris (Lord Nuffield)

Looking back on the career of a prominent businessman one is tempted to remark how obvious and easy it was. In William Morris's case it was far from obvious. He came from a background similar to Lever's but owing to illness the family fortunes had declined. As a youth he was a racing cyclist and from pedal cycles he became interested in motor cycles. He started on his own, repairing cycles and selling accessories, and in 1893 with a capital of £4 he began to build his own machines. In 1900 by using bought castings he built a single-cylinder 1¾ h.p. engine which he fitted into a cycle frame. He took in a working partner who had been a close friend on the track. The partnership broke up after a year as, like Lever's early partners, Joseph Cooper was too hesitant about the risks. He tried a three-man partnership, the other two being an undergraduate with money and an Oxford businessman with a number of shops. The former spent money lavishly and the business failed. Once more Morris had to start again.

He learned the lesson, to be independent and to rely on his own efforts. He resumed business under his own name and extended into motor cars, and Morris Garages sold and repaired cars, ran a car-hire business and a driving school. So far there was nothing different from the many small garage owners who were becoming established in the new trade. But in 1912 he decided to go into motor manufacture. There were many small manufacturers, generally engineers who made the car of their choice and endeavoured to sell it at a profit and to remain in business. Generally they tended to make all the car themselves. Morris, perhaps luckily, had neither the capital nor the production facilities to make the car himself. He also expected to get lower prices if he went to specialist producers for components.

It was usual to wait until after the Motor Show before manufacturers gave orders to suppliers. Morris worked on the basis of planned production before he had received an order. He planned on the basis that he would sell 1,500 units of his model, a two-seater 8·9 h.p. car for £169, and was successful in getting suppliers to tool up to supply him. He was able to convince other manufacturers that he was worth backing, and unlike his early experience in direct partnership, he always seemed to be able to find a number of people to help him in various ways, especially financial.

During the war he had experience in the volume production of mine sinkers for the Admiralty and this taught him that 'efficient production could be achieved by quite small suppliers when their products were carefully designed from the point of view of the final assembly and when they were supplied with the necessary jigs and other equipment.'[10] By 1921 he established a leadership in the motor industry; he brought his prices down, he lowered costs through a large volume of production, and even by standardising parts, brought lower costs to the industry as a whole. The basis of the Cowley works was buying, not manufacturing, and Morris assembled a carefully thought out mass of specialised components. (Marks and Spencer also 'assembles' in the shops the components of the clothing requirements of the housewife.) If it all appears too easy and obvious with hindsight, it must be emphasised that by 1913 as many as 198 different makes had been put on the market and 103 had dropped out, and 81 cars made in 1920 had disappeared by 1928.

Of the engineering firms Rolls-Royce survived at the high-price quality end of the market where most of the customers, embassies and heads of state and leading businessmen, bought prestige, generally with other people's money. The 'Wedgwood' of the car industry, (Sir) William Lyons at Jaguar, built up Jaguar cars by providing something in between, a high-powered family saloon at a price for value which amazed the industry. It was built on the development of a racing engine which had powered different types of cars for many years.

It can't happen now

Many people will say that this is all very well but these examples are from the past, and it cannot happen today, what with the large corporation, income tax, death duties, the government, trade unions, large-scale production, monopoly or competition, or anything else – business expansion from small beginnings is impossible. This was being said when Morris first started, and he stated that similar opportunities to his existed in many other branches of industry, and that he often felt tempted to use his methods in some of the more backward areas of British management. Of course, all examples are historical, because once they have happened they are part of history and one must wait a certain period to see whether a new firm or new venture is successful or not.

Even in the face of the established firms new competitors may arise in different ways. One of the little-noted instances of 'entrepreneurial' ability occurred between the wars. The nineteenth century had seen the establishment of the railways as the principal method of inland transport – a highly capitalised, entrenched monopoly, based on the steam engine and the fixed rail. The invention of the internal combustion engine changed all that. After the First World War there was a large number of ex-servicemen who had been taught to drive, and who had a little capital from gratuities, a number of ex-army vehicles for disposal, and a lack of other opportunities. Hundreds of new firms were established either to carry goods, or to break into new passenger markets where the poor could get a cheap charabanc ride to the sea, or country districts could be serviced adequately for the first time. This development was so successful that the vested interests were able in the 1930s to pass legislation, by licensing and other devices, to limit the effect of the new invention. It was said at the time that it was difficult to throw a stone at the Conservative benches without hitting a railway director, and on the other side the railway unions were well represented

But one of the remarkable features of postwar Britain has been the very large number of businesses which have made a public issue of shares, and some of these were set up since the war. In many cases the 'par' for the first million pounds appears to be about fifteen to seventeen years. (The special reasons for 'going public' are examined in chapter 3 below.) A few examples will illustrate the point.

Demetrius Comino had a successful little printing business and needed some kind of easy storage equipment. With £7,000 drawn from the printing business he founded Dexion in 1947 making slotted angle equipment and by 1961 the company employed 1,200 people.

The Solartron Electronic Group was started in 1947 in a disused stable by two engineers with a few hundred pounds' capital. It was later joined by another with both capital and administrative ability. In six years turnover increased fourteen times and in 1959 it sold out to an industrial holding company, Firth Cleveland.

John James learnt about wireless in the RAF and with his gratuity and savings rented a shop in Bristol in 1946. By the time he had expanded it to over 300 shops he sold the business also to Firth Cleveland for £5·8 million, half in cash and half in shares, and joined the parent company board.

Coseley Buildings was started by three partners in a wooden shed with a capital of £10,000 and in twelve years reached a turnover of over £3 million. In 1947 David Kaye bought a second-hand car and started selling birthday cards. Later with two partners and a capital of £500 he founded Kaye-Gibson. By 1963 the turnover was £3 million and he had a staff of 700. Buxted Chicken was started by Andrew Fisher with a hundred chicks in a loose box. It became a public company in 1960 with 600 employees.

Kenneth Wood set up Kenwood in 1947 with £800 capital in a small workshop to make the Kenwood Electric Chef. If he had listened to the market-research specialists he would never have ventured. The success of one product led to others, smaller mixers, steam irons, fan heaters, etc. A new factory was built at Havant and by 1961 1,760 people were employed.[11]

Colin Chapman started in the high-performance car business in 1952 with a borrowed capital of £25. In 1968 his Lotus Cars was valued at over £8 million when the company went public. In another industry dominated by large firms and price rings (Sir) Jules Thorn in 1928 broke into the electric lamp market. From lighting, the firm went into radio and television, often importing against the established maker before starting its own factory.

The sight of holiday-makers sitting in the rain gave (Sir) William Butlin the idea for his holiday camps and the first was set up in 1935. The established catering trade was broken into with the idea of a good steak served in a comfortable atmosphere; Berni Inns developed the principle after the war of offering a limited and standardised menu, which meant that staff could be trained quickly. The same principle has been developed by Angus Steak Houses and Golden Egg, and has contributed to the closing of the Corner Houses of the Lyons group. With the changed social habits and with more people eating out, the restaurant business offers scope for people with fresh ideas, such as Old Kentucky Restaurants which went public in 1968 after ten years' trading.

But the biggest rush of all came with property development. In the nineteenth century there were firms such as Cubitt, which built Belgravia, Bloomsbury and Pimlico, and had the same reputation for excellence as Brassey. After the war, building had been controlled and restricted by the Town and Country Planning Act of 1947 and other measures. When the restrictions were removed in 1954 the floodgates opened. Capital from banks for bridging loans, money from the institutional investors such as insurance companies seeking something better than the 'cheap money' investments available after the war, the great demand for new buildings, all created an economic climate in which over a hundred people became millionaires in a short time.[12]

Some businesses survive and expand, others are like bubbles which blow up and burst. This will be considered in the next two chapters.

Notes

1 The full story of this business, and of many others to be considered, is well documented in general and specialist studies, some of which are to be found in the Guide to further reading. It is not my purpose here to repeat the history of the Industrial Revolution, but to examine only those features that are relevant to this particular study.

2 Andrew Ure, *The Philosophy of Manufactures*, H. Bohn, 1835.

3 Samuel Smiles, *Industrial Biography*.

4 Even today, those who are prominent in the affairs of their trade associations are not always in the forefront of the successful businessmen.

5 A. E. Musson, 'James Nasmyth and the early growth of mechanical engineering', *Economic History Review*, vol. x, 1957–8.
6 N. McKendrick, 'Josiah Wedgwood, an eighteenth century entrepreneur in salesmanship and marketing techniques', *Economic History Review*, vol. xii, no. 3, April 1960.
7 R. S. Lambert, *The Universal Provider*.
8 Lambert, op. cit., p. 152.
9 Charles Wilson, *The History of Unilever*.
10 P. W. S. Andrews and Elizabeth Brunner, *The Life of Lord Nuffield*, p. 87. It is perhaps necessary to remind younger readers that William Morris became Lord Nuffield.
11 Harry Miller, *The Way of Enterprise*, André Deutsch, 1963.
12 Oliver Marriott, *The Property Boom*, Hamish Hamilton, 1967.

Two

The sons of the fathers – business continuation

> The maintenance of a high standard of leadership in any industry is sometimes more difficult than the attainment of leadership in the first place.
>
> Alfred P. Sloan, *My Years with General Motors*, p. 22[1]

Even successful entrepreneurs are mortal, and unless each generation is to start afresh with a new business when the founder dies, there must be some continuation. There are certain obvious examples of long-lived businesses; the Bank of England was established in 1694, many insurance companies are nearly as old, and the Hudson's Bay Company was given its charter by Charles II with Prince Rupert as its first governor, and 'the governor and company of adventurers of England' still trade in furs and stores in Canada.

The normal pattern is that the founder builds up a business for the benefit of himself and his family and expects his son to carry on where he leaves off. If the latter is lucky his own son succeeds him. This presupposes that he has a son or sons to succeed him, and that they have sufficient ability to keep the business alive. But the 'normal' may be statistically abnormal. There are many possible and actual variations from this pattern. The inheritance may not be in the direct line. The business may go to nephews or even more distant relatives in large families; or the business may be sold by the widow or other heirs, and a new family takes over and perhaps solves the succession problem. It is a moot point whether we say that the business has continued under new ownership, or whether we say that it has failed and been carried on by the purchasers. Of course all businesses are in different hands – the original founders are all dead – and the distinction between those continued by blood relations and those taken over by new entrepreneurs is probably not of great importance. But if the business is sold to a larger organisation, which is very common today, in general we can state that it has failed; failed in the sense that it has not been continued as a separate enterprise although in another sense it may have been very successful and the vendors may have done very well out of the sale. The special case of failure to operate will be treated in the next chapter.

To some extent the sons of the fathers are 'on to a good hiding for nothing'. If they succeed in extending the business, or even just in keeping it going, this will be attributed to influence and to the effect of the silver spoon. If they fail they will be compared unfavourably with the father. Yet the inheritors cannot be blamed if they fail to manage what is really an unmanageable group: the founder was often unable to manage it himself. Even if the portrait of the 'old man' is not glowering at him from the boardroom walls, the son must have the uneasy feeling that people are waiting for the chance to say 'I told you so'. The British believe in the hereditary principle when applied to racehorses but are apt to distrust it when applied to business.

The benefit that the son has, besides inheriting a going business, is the training that the father can give him, especially if the growth period corresponds with his own attainment of maturity. He sees the business grow and gets the opportunity to understand it thoroughly. The disadvantage, in some cases, is that if the founder is a very strong, independent character, as so many of them are, the son may never get the opportunity for any independent judgment. The founder trusts no one, not even his own family. Henry Ford's son tried to escape from his father's clutches. As he died before his father, the business came down to the grandson, Henry Ford II, who had to be brought out of the navy to manage the business. In spite of the opportunities put in his way by the establishment of the firm of Robert Stephenson and Co., Robert went mining in South America to escape from George Stephenson. It was perhaps fortunate that the mining venture failed and Robert came back to the family business – after having made his point and asserted his independence. Edward VII even when past middle age was never trusted by Queen Victoria to see state papers and learn his craft.

Although blood is thicker than water and there may be a strong unifying potential in the family business, family quarrels and disagreements are often much greater because the members cannot get away from each other so easily. The political dynastic solution of assassination is not readily available.

Without going into the controversy of heredity versus environment it is true that there are families which produce an array of talent which breaks out in all walks of life. (The process of ennoblement which accompanies success and the conferment of a different title conceals the family 'name' and family relationship to all except the assiduous readers of *Debrett.*) It is often surprising to learn, for example, that some prominent lady of today is the granddaughter of a Victorian notability. Native talent comes out in all sorts of ways; it is to be expected therefore that it will occur in business.

The comparison between the founder and the later generation may be unfair to the latter. The founder, as we have seen, gets in with some new idea or with the exploitation of an invention. The firm expands with the expansion of the industry and the new conditions are so easy that only the most incompetent management could fail to prosper. In time the expansion period is over, one cannot go on plastering the countryside with new type blast furnaces or covering it with an endless supply of railway lines. The industry reaches maturity. One firm can expand only at the expense of another's failure; in Marshall's famous analogy, the forest remains the same, while individual trees may grow, reach maturity, and decay – or like the elms be struck down by outside factors. The firms may survive for generations, without any spectacular events in their history, but they continue to earn profits by supplying the goods and services to the consumers in the market. To consolidate and survive is business success.

The Siemens family in Germany produced eight sons, of whom only one was not prominent in industry. Two founded the great Dresden glassworks, three developed the international telegraph industry, cable making and the electrical industry. It was an offshoot of this firm which founded Siemens Brothers in Britain in 1858. It was later absorbed in AEI.[2]

The Geddes dynasty has made its mark in modern industry. One cousin became managing director of Dunlop, another chairman of Limmer and Trinidad Lake and another reached the top of P and O. Each is the son of famous fathers, Sir Eric as chairman of Dunlop and Imperial Airways, the first Lord Geddes who went from surgery to politics and the City, and Sir Aukland in the family shipping interests. Reputations were acquired in other ways. Lord Geddes became the country's leading tanker expert with Shell and the Admiralty before joining P and O. Mr Reay Geddes went first to the Bank of England after reading economics at Cambridge before going on to Dunlop. While being a Geddes has helped, it is not enough. They are three out of thirteen cousins.[3]

David Brown, the grandfather of the present chairman, started in 1860 to serve the Yorkshire woollen industry and the same family firm is now a large manufacturer of machine tools, gears and tractors. Arthur Guinness started brewing in 1759 and by a combination of salesmanship and quality and concentration on the one thing the company could do best not only dominated the Irish industry but forced its products into the 'tied house' system of Britain without having had to acquire its own public houses.

After the death of Michael Marks, Marks and Spencer ran into difficulties, and Simon Marks and Israel Sieff (related by marriage) had a long struggle to get on to the board, and to have the opportunity to build the modern business. The long life of the London shops, many in family control, such as Heals, Maples, Debenhams, Peter Robinson, Fortnum and Mason, is well known. Harrods was under two Harrods but three Burbidges.

There has been a similar pattern in the steel industry. In the last century working-class men with no capital could go into partnership with people with money to invest; John Vaughan was the son of an iron worker, Thomas Brown the same, and Thomas Knowles the son of a colliery overman. Quick profits in a new product which required little initial capital gave the funds which allowed the Firth brothers, Samuel Fox and William Barningham to engage in heavy steel manufacture. Since then 'the steel industry has been governed to a large extent by dynastic heirs or investors. Family men are predominant. Frequently the family which continues into the third or fourth generation is not that of the founders but a family of later investors.'[4]

An interesting case of the family business is that of Bessemer. He invented a method of making bronze powder cheaply. He met Mr Young, the inventor of the type-composing machine who proposed to provide the necessary capital for a share in the profits. The idea was relatively simple and if it had been patented it could have been easily copied by others. Also workmen could soon obtain a knowledge of the process and pass it on, so Bessemer decided to keep the whole process secret. He himself made complete working drawings of all the machines to be used, and had the parts made by different manufacturers so that none of them would know the purpose and operation of the machines. To allow three people to do the work of seventy to eighty workmen the machines had to be designed on what Bessemer called the principle of the 'self acting machine', a machine that would take care of itself, perform the work and throw itself out of gear when the work was completed. (He did not call the process 'automation'!)

But to preserve the secret he engaged his wife's three younger brothers at high salaries, and the family operated machinery which would have required a large number of workmen. The secret was kept for forty years. When he later invented the Bessemer converter he had to take out a patent as his ideas had been published. He formed a sort of 'business family' by selling a licence to operate to one firm only in each district, to bind them closer to him and to make them supporters of the patent, among whom were H. A. Bruce (Lord Aberdare) of Dowlais, the Govan Iron Works of Glasgow, and the old-established Butterley Iron Company. It is perhaps significant that only the ironmasters were interested and the steel masters turned down an idea which revolutionised steel making. Bessemer in his autobiography pays tribute to those whose scrupulous honesty had made his business a success. One of the brothers-in-law, W. D. Allen, became managing partner of Henry Bessemer and Co. of Sheffield and he eventually bought out the works after fourteen years when Bessemer and the other partners retired. One of them was an architect employed by the firm, who became a partner and Bessemer's brother-in-law. Richard Allen was given the bronze business; but the third had died before Bessemer retired.

Nathan Mayer Rothschild was one of five brothers sent out into the leading money centres of the world, London, Paris, Vienna, Frankfurt and Naples. He founded the London house in 1804. N. M. Rothschild and Sons (and sons and sons and nephews) has been prominent in banking ever since. Its predominant position declined after the First World War but since the Second there has been a revival in its fortunes. It is still dominated by family members and one of the interwar problems was that all the family talents were not directed towards banking. Members made their mark in other walks of life. Since the war non-family members have been admitted to partnership. During the nineteenth century its idea was that international finance and investment centred on the London Money Market, which was little concerned with home finance. The loss of the predominating position of sterling reduced the partnership's activities, but it survived. Since the war it has adapted to the new role of the merchant banker as a provider of finance in the home trade.

Baring Brothers, also founded by immigrants in the eighteenth century, followed the same pattern of overseas finance. It underwent a very sticky passage in 1890 but survived. Family members under different names – those of the titles conferred – contribute to banking, finance, politics and public affairs.

The Pease family of Darlington provided the banker's backing for the Stockton and Darlington railway, and was prominent in railway management (the LNER) for well over a hundred years. The banking partnership continued until 1902, when as a result of getting into financial difficulties it was transferred to Barclays Bank. This bank itself was created in 1896 by a combination of Quaker banking firms, many of them interrelated by marriage, all with a long tradition of family banking – Barclays, Gurneys, Backhouses, Tukes, etc. It was a branch of the Barclay family which bought the brewery renamed Barclay Perkins. Lloyds Bank has a similar origin in interconnected Quaker families; here the other interest is not brewing, but the iron trade; the Lloyd of Stewarts and Lloyds is of the same origin.[5]

There is the contrast in adaptability to the market. Mudie's Select Library (a high-class lending library) was founded in 1842 and for about fifty years enjoyed an unchallenged position. But it was unable to adapt to the change to cheaper books, the rise of the periodical and the cheap newspaper, and went out of business in 1937. Whereas W. H. Smith, founded before 1792, and managed by five generations of the Smith family, prospered on the rise of the daily newspaper and the railway bookstall. It went public after the Second World War only because its success raised the problem of estate duties on the family fortunes.

The early steam engines built by Boulton and Watt were often constructed locally where they were used, and the firm relied on the royalties from their twenty-five-year patent granted by Act of Parliament. They acted as consulting engineers and designers rather than as manufacturers of the steam engine. There were other manufacturing partnerships in Boulton's multifarious activities, but these did not concern the engine.

The patent expired in 1800 bringing an end to further royalty income. The early customers had been in the mining industries of Cornwall and the midlands, and in the former especially, with the special type of cost-book mining partnerships, the provision of pumping equipment under a royalty agreement suited their purpose. But a new range of opportunity opened up with the application of steam power instead of the water-wheel to the expanding cotton manufacturers. The mill owners preferred to purchase the machinery outright; Boulton and Watt therefore had to go into direct manufacture on their own account, or face the fact that the impetus of their invention would fizzle out. A new Soho foundry was built for engine manufacture.

The two sons of the founders, James Watt junior and Matthew Robinson Boulton, had been given a good education by their parents and were partners in other family businesses. They had been brought up together and got on well with one another – the ideal partnership. The first Boulton and Watt were elderly and Watt wished to retire, so the new enterprise was the work of the sons.

An excellent site was chosen close to a canal for the transport of heavy equipment. The foundry was completed in three months, with wharf, foundry cranes, movable triangular crane, engine, blowing apparatus, lathes, drills and all necessary equipment. The plans gave details of the work to be performed by each machine and operating standards were laid down. The foundry was laid out so that work could follow the best route through the factory (the principle of 'routeing') and a costing system was put into practice. There was, in the words of Professor J. G. Smith,[6]

> nothing in the details of the most progressive factory practice of today that the two sons had not anticipated. Neither Taylor, Ford, nor other modern experts devised anything in the way of plan that cannot be discovered at Soho before 1805; and the Soho system of costing is superior to that employed in very many successful concerns today. This earliest engineering factory, therefore, possessed an organisation on the management side which was not excelled even by the technical skill of the craftsmen it produced.

Their achievements, however, did not include the provision of successors; the firm gradually declined and in 1895 the firm of James Watt and Co. was sold to W. and T. Avery. We owe much of our knowledge of the firm to the fact that Avery had the good sense to preserve the old records they found on taking over.

A less harmonious picture is presented of the Crawshay family. The founder of the business, Richard Crawshay, began in an iron warehouse in London and bought himself into partnership in the iron works at Cyfarthfa. He wielded great power in the Welsh iron industry and became known as the 'King of Merthyr'. He was succeeded by the first William Crawshay. His 'business' was of a most peculiar structure. He was in partnership in Wales with some people, and with quite different people in the London warehouse, which was generally the selling outlet for the iron. There were strong differences of opinion over policy, especially that of tying the London warehouse to purchases of iron from William's other partnership in Cyfarthfa. For example, he was in partnership with one of his sons in one business, and the two of them were in partnership with another son and other people in another. The Crawshay business was in reality two separate businesses but both had as their connecting link the one strong-minded man. The only way in which William could bring sense and unity into the business was to reduce his sons and other partners to the status of salaried assistants under his sole direction. But autocratic as he was, he drew the line at this. He did make a change in the partnership arrangements whereby each member held some interest in the different concerns and a measure of unity was achieved. The same conflict of interests can occur where a holding company trades with subsidiary companies which are not wholly owned, and the terms upon which inter-company trade is undertaken may be detrimental to the interests of the minority shareholders in the subsidiary companies. There have been a number of complaints since the war of the treatment of minorities where a takeover has acquired control without complete ownership.

On the death of the first William most of his business passed to the second son, also William – presumably recognising the principle of inheritance to the most able and not that of primogeniture. All the jealousies and mistrust of the old arrangements were revived, and the three brothers quarrelled bitterly. It took many years of dispute before the business was unified under the younger William.

The Quaker Darby firm had different men and a very different history. When the famous Abraham Darby, the elder, the man who developed at Coalbrookdale the method of smelting iron by using coke instead of the increasingly scarce charcoal, died in 1717 his eldest son was only six years old. The widow had to assign eight shares in the business to Thomas Golding, a Bristol merchant who held a mortgage from Darby; two she sold to her son-in-law, Richard Ford, and six went to another man who claimed a debt on the estate. In 1718 a new partnership was set up. Golding held the largest number of shares, but the feature of the arrangement was that Joshua Sergeant held three shares for the children of Darby, and Ford held two. The three of them managed the business. Golding became the financial agent, banker and selling agent for Bristol and the south-west; Ford, with the title of clerk, managed the works and visited fairs in the midlands and the north. Ford was a capable man of business and had been trained by his father-in-law. Besides his technical improvements he developed the sales side not only in England but he also created a great export trade through the Bristol merchants. A well-known product with a large market in Africa was the three-legged cauldron, which still survives in cartoons of missionaries being boiled for dinner!

When Ford had managed for twelve years the younger son, also Abraham Darby, now nineteen years old and having been trained in the works, was given a regular position as Ford's assistant (Ford was his uncle). He was later admitted to the partnership and the division of labour was organised so that Ford concentrated on the selling side and Abraham on the technical. He became works manager although Golding and Ford still held thirteen-sixteenths of the shares. Golding's shares eventually passed to his relatives who had policy control. This is why the firm undertook gun production although this was contrary to Quaker principles. When Ford died in 1745 the management passed to Abraham Darby, and Richard Ford's son became clerk to the firm.

More talent came into the business through marriage. Richard Reynolds learnt his trade in Bristol by being apprenticed to a grocer, William Fry – a cousin of the Joseph Fry who founded the chocolate firm. Reynolds's father was an iron merchant and bought from Coalbrookdale; Reynolds was sent by Golding to the works to transact some business for him and there he met and married the daughter of the second Abraham Darby. He went into one of the firm's foundries with capital provided by his father. Abraham Darby on his death in 1763 left a son too young to manage the business and Reynolds moved to Coalbrookdale to act as manager of the whole works. He was in the Darby tradition, an excellent technical manager and innovator, and was much concerned for the well-being of the workmen, and continued the policy of providing houses for employees.

In 1768 the third Abraham Darby, at the age of eighteen, took over the management, with the assistance of Reynolds and the older workmen. It was the third Darby who built the famous iron bridge over the Severn, and the firm did work for Boulton and Watt, providing cylinders for the engines, and were customers of the firm for steam pumps.

One remarkable feature of the business was that the first four generations were short lived and the managers took over at a young age: the father Abraham Darby at thirty, Ford at twenty-eight, the son Abraham Darby at twenty-one, Reynolds at twenty-seven, the grandson Abraham Darby at eighteen, Edmund Darby (a nephew of the third Darby) at twenty-one, a fourth Abraham Darby at twenty-three, and Alfred Darby also at twenty-three. The other is that when the sons were too young to succeed in the dynasty, it was the sons-in-law who took over the management, and never ousted the heirs from their inheritance. Marriage brought in more talent and honesty. Gradually the family retired from the business and there was no Darby in active management after 1850, although the names occur among the directors of the subsequent company.[8]

Another Quaker iron firm has a similar history with an important diversion at the end. Ambrose Crowley was sent by his father, a Stourbridge ironmonger, to be apprenticed in London. After setting up in business on his own account he quarrelled with the midland suppliers of ironware and decided to set up in business as a manufacturer, first at Sunderland and later at Winlaton and in other areas. His early factory system was an outstanding example of a new organisation, combining direct work with the then more normal outwork. As he operated the business from London (goods coming by sea from his factories) he laid down a series of instruction manuals for his various officials – *The Law Book of the Crowley Ironworks* – which were well in advance of his time (see below, chapter 5). He died in 1713, and his business was carried on by his son John. On the latter's death in 1728 at the early age of thirty-eight, the business was carried on by John's widow, Theodosia.[9]

> Her widowhood lasted 54 years. During most of this time she directed what was claimed to be the largest ironworks in Europe, managed the large landed estates which the wealth of her husband and father-in-law had accumulated, successively married off her several daughters into the ranks of the aristocracy and retained a prominent place in the fashionable circles of Mayfair and Bath.

Her sons died young; Ambrose and John took some part in the management but she survived them both.

The daughters who were married into the aristocracy brought with them considerable dowries – probably their main attraction, the 'plump Crowley's'[10] money was irresistible. The Earl of Ashburnham probably netted about £200,000. On the death of Theodosia the main ownership passed into his hands, and that of Charles Boone who had married another daughter. The 'owners' had no interest in the business, apart from the financial rewards, and the business was carried on by a succession of managers in the Millington family until it finally collapsed in 1863. The Darby daughters brought talent into the family business, the Crowley daughters caused money to flow out.[11]

Robert Owen got his introduction to David Dale at the New Lanark Mills by marrying Dale's daughter; Arnold Weinstock married into the Sobel Wireless Company and with his father-in-law revitalised the business; Louis Cohen married the daughter of David Lewis, the founder of Lewis's stores; the daughter of Jack Cohen of Tesco married Hyman Kreitman, who as chief executive fills the place that could have gone to a son; and there are many other firms where relatives by marriage occupy important positions on the board.

Sometimes, where the talent is running out a business is revitalised from outside; the Burbidge dynasty and Harrods has already been mentioned; Isaac Wolfson moved into an ailing company and built up Great Universal Stores; Lord Woolton as a young man was a great friend of one of the younger Cohens, and he eventually managed Lewis's; and when Sobel was taken over by GEC that company acquired Weinstock who rose to the top due to natural talent. Burtons acquired Jackson the Tailors, largely with the object of providing for future management, but the company still seems to be searching for succession.

The passing or retirement of the more glamorous postwar entrepreneurs has meant that the sons have the opportunity; Butlin handed over to his son, and the death of Sir Hugh Fraser gave a large empire to his son; and the Clark brothers, after a very hard training by the father, are directing Plessey.

But no pattern emerges. The long-lasting firms have either produced a line that is able – and willing – to manage the family business, or they have married ability, or even brought it in almost by accident from outside. But even in some of the large public companies there is often a very strong family influence which is much greater than would be justified by the shareholding alone.

Notes

1 Alfred P. Sloan, *My Years with General Motors*, Pan Books, 1969.
2 J. D. Scott, *Siemens Brothers 1858–1958*, Weidenfeld and Nicolson, 1958.
3 'Observer', *Financial Times*, 24 April 1964.
4 Charlotte Erickson, *British Industrialists. Steel and Hosiery, 1850–1950.*
5 Paul H. Emden, *Quakers in Commerce*, Sampson Low, Marston, 1939. There is also much interesting information on other firms, where the Quakers were often interrelated by marriage, such as John Bright in cotton, Allen and Hanbury in pharmacy, Bryant and May in matches, Huntley and Palmer in biscuits, the Frys, Rowntrees and Cadburys in chocolate, and their influence on banking and early railway building.
6 Quoted in Eric Roll, *An Early Experiment in Industrial Organisation.*
7 John P. Addis, *The Crawshay Dynasty.*
8 Arthur Raistrick, *Dynasty of Ironfounders.*
9 M. W. Flinn, *The Law Book of the Crowley Ironworks* and *Men of Iron.*
10 They were objects of ridicule in some of the Restoration dramas.
11 M. W. Flinn, op. cit.

Three

Clogs to clogs – business failure

> Some fifty years ago when I first became connected with industry, I found myself associated with firms managed by the men who had founded them, and although there were notable exceptions, these men on the whole were full of vigour and enterprise, they had confidence in themselves and more than that they were anxious to exploit new ideas, not on the 'get-rich-quick' ticket, but to establish good, solid, industrial undertakings that would be of lasting value and a credit to themselves and the country. Now things are totally different.
>
> P. W. Kingsford, *F. W. Lanchester*

It is proverbial that business families go from clogs to clogs (or shirt sleeves to shirt sleeves) in three generations. A common explanation of this phenomenon is that the business is founded by the sort of entrepreneur we have seen in chapter 1. While the son who succeeds him may or may not have the same energy and drive, he was brought up in the business when it was expanding, he probably started in the business from the bottom by helping his father and had a thorough knowledge of the firm and the industry. His education was in the business. By the time the third generation is there to succeed, conditions have changed. The grandson is born into easier circumstances. He was probably given a 'good education' to confer a certain social cachet on the family. He never had the same struggles – or the same excitement. He is less enterprising and the business goes down.

There is some truth in this picture. In that other family business, hereditary monarchy, three passably good kings in succession are rare. But ruin in three generations must be regarded as a special case only among many others. Chapter 2 disproves this being a general rule; there are many businesses which are thriving and prosperous in their fifth and sixth generation of family management.

There is, however, a variation of this dictum which may be nearer the general truth, 'shirt sleeves to bishop's gaiters or barrister's wig in three generations'. In the third generation the different education and background may mean that the grandsons use their patrimony to enter the professions, away from the family business. The control may be left to the relative who is not averse to a business career, or even to a professional manager, with the inheritors exercising a fairly weak control through being members of the board of directors. Sometimes at moments of stress they have had to be called in from their more interesting professional activities to revitalise the family business. The talent is still there but the holders of it have other interests than the business. It is in reserve if necessary. While the American ideal may be 'log cabin to White House' in the same generation, in Britain it can be Scottish croft to Downing Street in three generations.

It is one thing to be rich by making money in business; it is quite different to have that money by inheritance. There has always been the tendency for accumulated wealth to be put into land, to found an estate as well as a dynasty – to move away from the ironworks or the glue factory or the mill into the shires of the squires. Defoe, in his *Tour through the Whole Island of Great Britain*, noted this with approval. Everywhere he went he asked about the ownership of 'the house' or the mansion, and was pleased when he was told it was in the hands of a retired London merchant. But great estates can be a cause of great expenses, and it is in this way that family fortunes can decline.

Again, we must not take this too literally. The business may go down without the entrepreneur being impoverished. It may be smaller than it was in its greatest days but still may provide a modest competence. He may have no intention, or opportunity, of founding a dynasty. If there is no one to succeed the best thing is to sell out. This may take the form of selling the entire business as it stands to a large firm which is expanding by purchase or takeover, and seeks new ideas or initiative by buying it. Or the selling may take the form of converting to a public company and floating part of the share capital, while still retaining managerial control for a time. In extreme cases, the former policy means selling out in time and in the latter going public before going bankrupt.

First-generation failure

When some prominent businessman is referred to as a Napoleon of industry it must be remembered that Napoleon had his Elba and after a comeback, his St Helena.[1]

From 1876, the year Lipton opened his first shop, to 1898, when the business was converted into a public company with a share capital of £2 million, the business had grown to 242 branches and twelve Ceylon tea estates ('tea from our own plantations'). It also manufactured cocoa, chocolate, confectionery, jam, marmalade, preserves, biscuits and beef extract for its own shops. In addition there were 3,300 specially appointed agencies in the United Kingdom, as well as agencies in thirty-eight countries. The prospectuses of 1908, 1919 and 1921 showed increasing trade and profits, and apart from no dividend in 1915 and 1916, profits and dividends expanded. From 1918 to 1923 12½ per cent was paid and in 1924 10 per cent, but nothing in the next three years.

In the 1926 report it was stated that an exhaustive inquiry was being undertaken into the business, which had not yet borne fruit. Preference dividends were in arrears and the profits failed to cover the debenture interest. In the 1927 report the company pointed out that a complete reorganisation and modernisation of branches and factories was necessary. This was not an easy task. Sir Thomas Lipton, who was still in control, expressed a desire to be relieved of all active management of the business, and he was created life president and chairman of the company. In 1929 there was a capital reorganisation and writing down of assets, which exceeded the value of the ordinary shares, so some of the cost fell on the preference shareholders who received 70 per cent of the equity as compensation. (Out of £4,423,765 total capital, £1,445,620 was represented by 'goodwill' which was obviously non-existent.)

The business had been in the same hands all its life, and the hands had faltered. In his later years Lipton had paid less attention to the company and devoted much of his time to yacht racing and the social cachet which this brought. The result was that he did not manage the company, and had not allowed anyone else to do so. There was no one in the firm to replace him. An arrangement was made with the Meadow Dairy Company, which had a similar business to Lipton but a different profit record, in which the Meadow took over the management of Lipton's, but with the secrecy of company accounts at that time no details were given.

Selfridge in his time made the same impact on the business scene as had Lipton in an earlier period, and had an even less fortunate ending. He also was a great socialite and his election night parties with 'name gathering' were famous. He was a brilliant salesman but his fundamental errors were financial miscalculation and *folie de grandeur*. Because he had been so successful he embarked on ventures beyond his powers and these brought him down.

The old-established business of William Whiteley, 'the Universal Provider', had gradually tapered off in his own lifetime. Other traders began to undercut him and after his murder the business was unprogressive. Selfridge bought control of Whiteley's in 1927. Such was his confidence in his managerial ability, and his belief that under his management the Whiteley business would recover its former glory, that Selfridge guaranteed for a period of twelve years the maintenance of certain dividends on Whiteley shares at the current rate.

The Whiteley profits, however, were insufficient to pay this dividend and Selfridges had to meet the guarantee. As Selfridge explained to the shareholders in the 1929 report: 'This is one of the temporary penalties of acquiring an old business which has demanded an enormous amount of effort in being reconstructed and brought reasonably up to date. This investment will eventually and before long prove a splendid asset to this house, but we have to go through a certain amount of loss before reaching a period of profit.' It was typical of the man that the transfer was made by reducing the normal depreciation in the accounts, and not by any reduction in dividends. The penalty did not prove temporary and Whiteley's was the running sore that depleted Selfridges' profits.

A similar dividend guarantee was made with another business venture, Selfridges Provincial Stores. This was a group of moderate-sized provincial and suburban shops that had been bought, with the object of bringing the trading methods of the main store to these other shops. But it is difficult to see how a method of trading which was suitable for a very large shop could be applied to other shops which were much too small to carry the variety of goods. It proved a failure. Moreover, there was a vast building programme at the Oxford Street store, and the high cost was never repaid by commensurate profits. When the main store suffered a reduction in income the guarantees drained off cash which was necessary for the survival of the firm. A further drain was the very large loan to the managing director (Selfridge) which he stated was due to the 'unhappy income tax'.

In 1940 Selfridge and his son retired from the board, and in 1945 he had to sever all connection with the company he had founded and built up, without settling the balance on the loan account. It was necessary for Selfridges to discontinue the connection with Whiteley's and to undertake a considerable writing off of capital. In the end, there was the pathetic spectacle of the old man walking in Oxford Street, and not being allowed to enter the store.

In the 1950s John Bloom found the almost perfect idea for quick expansion. He could buy a Dutch washing machine for £29, sell it for £44 and undercut all the well-known appliance makers by using mail order selling. An advertising expenditure of £437 brought in 8,000 replies and the machine was launched. At the peak, advertising expenditure was well over £1 million a year and all selling was done on commission following up the flood of replies to the national advertising. In the early days he bought his components, sold machines against orders and deposits, and was self-financing.

But the business got too large for these rather primitive methods. He required a permanent supply and had to go back to manufacture, and find other products to justify the extent of the empire. Everything that was done had the mark of apparent success and all the correct decisions appeared to be taken, and accepted by the pundits. To obtain a stock exchange quotation a 'reverse takeover' was made for the firm of Rolls Razor, a company with a good product which had fallen on hard times. The public issue was made on his behalf by a leading city issuing house; he made a deal with the Pressed Steel Company which was having difficulty in selling its refrigerators, by which Bloom was to apply his selling ability to Pressed Steel's refrigerators, while Pressed Steel would manufacture washing machines at their Swansea factory. Two directors of Pressed Steel joined the Rolls Razor board, which provided manufacturing expertise, and Bloom went on the board of a subsidiary of Pressed Steel. But that did not work out and the deal was unscrambled.

Bloom had his washing machines made at the works of Sir Charles Colston and the latter joined the R-R board. This was a 'catch'. Colston before the war had been the force behind the British subsidiary of Hoover, and knew all about the selling problems of expensive consumer durables. On his retirement he founded a company and was producing a dishwasher. A joint company was set up, but this venture did not endure either. The dishwasher was a long-term market and the much younger man had not the patience to wait.

The finance of the hire-purchase business was made through Drages, a subsidiary of Great Universal Stores, and even to be associated, if only by implication, with Sir Isaac Wolfson, was virtually a financial guarantee, especially when Wolfson stated that in Bloom he saw himself thirty years previously.

Attempts were made to market other lines of goods, such as do-it-yourself central heating kits, cheap deep freezes, and a range of cosmetics. A number of discount shops were set up. None of these proved to be successful. The washing machine competitors, shaken out of their duopoly stupor, began to hit back, revise their efforts and cut their prices. It became increasingly difficult to sell the Bloom washing machines despite the large increase in advertising expenditure and all sorts of free inducements to purchasers, such as cut-price holidays in the Balkans. Eventually the bubble burst and after a brief meteoric rise the Rolls Razor company crashed in bankruptcy.

The whole operation had been based on the short-lived success of one product sold by intensive selling methods which were not as new as many people made out. The product became out of date with the development of the twin-tub machine, and no replacement or other product was found to be successful. On the credit side, the housewife got a cheap washing machine, both from Bloom and from the revitalised competitors, and the market in consumer durables was never the same again.

Cyril Lord, in addition to being a gifted salesman as are many people mentioned here, was an expert in the techniques of his product, carpets. He was recognised as such in the United States where he received an honorary doctorate for his contribution to textiles. According to the *Sunday Times* of 4 May 1969:

> Almost single-handed Lord had changed the entire character of the British carpet market, transforming it from a cottage industry to a mass market operation; he had built what was generally agreed to be Europe's largest and best equipped tufted carpet factory and he was selling more tufted carpet in an expanding field than any other single manufacturer.

After ten years of a rather erratic record the ordinary shares were offered to the public in 1964 and this was followed by record profits in 1966. Losses followed and by 1968 the business had collapsed. In its rise there had been the same adulation of a discovered genius as had witnessed the rise of Lipton, Selfridge and Bloom.

The main cause of the collapse was very similar: overexpansion into different fields or aspects of the business. He went into vinyl floor covering, in a market where Marley tiles were already well established and experienced. Lord made wider lengths and found technical difficulties in producing a satisfactory backing at that size. Marley's experience was that a covering that would not go into the boot of a car would not sell. Machines installed to make the extra-wide vinyl coverings were largely unused. After a visit to Russia he decided to manufacture artificial astrakhan with Russian machines without having undertaken any market research. When the firm crashed the machines had not produced a single item. An outdoor carpet, named Cyrilawn, failed to retain its green colour and was a failure.

But there was the common and fundamental mistake of integrating into a different type of trade. Shops were opened to sell the Lord carpets. These proved to be uneconomic as they would be competing with specialist carpet shops carrying a range of goods from many manufacturers, and the specialist department stores. Manufacturing expertise and retailing are two activities which often fail to blend successfully. Likwise the venture into hire-purchase finance, another highly specialised business, with the object of facilitating the sale of carpets, proved to be a loss maker.

Lack of management

Another common cause of first-generation failure – or partial failure – is the inability to establish a proper management of the business. (A definition of 'management', and its further consideration, will be deferred to chapters 7 and 8.) The one idea is pursued with vigour but there is no permanent basis for the company. This is particularly true where a large part of the growth in the size of the firm has come from acquisitions of other companies. A 'deal' may be arranged in a matter of days, and it is only then that the management problems start.

It is not that forceful entrepreneurs lack the will and the ability to manage; too often they 'manage' too much. Just because they are so able and know every detail of the business they have built up in their own lifetime, they regard their associates as inferior to them, which they often are, and so keep all the reins in their own hands and take all the decisions. Even if they wish to delegate to others their autocratic interference does little to foster true managerial ability among their subordinates. There is also the autocratic fault of distrusting good subordinate ability when it is present. The ruler must be seen to be the ruler and superior in all ways.

The difficulty is in going from stage 1, the entrepreneurial, to stage 2, the managerial. This is very clearly brought out in Charles Wilson's classic *The History of Unilever* (1954). According to Dr Wilson William Lever felt that 'his colleagues were men of more modest and ordinary talents . . . their cautious hesitancy was a constant irritation to him', and 'the art of delegating authority was one he never learned'. In the 1890s, at the height of his powers, he had

> [an] office with glass walls, practically the whole of the business was carried in his head and was directed by his verbal instructions. . . . From the office on the bridge came an unending stream of commands, prophecies, and exhortations. . . Autocracy was the essence of the system and woe betide the idle or the presumptuous. . . . Conversion into a public company did not shake in the slightest Lever's conviction that the business was his to control and that its successes were his own personal achievement

The original soap business had expanded by the acquisition of other, and older, soap companies, and in addition Lever's engaged in a variety of activities, some of which, for example, the creation of MacFisheries, were the personal whim of Lever. After the First World War some order had to be brought out of this managerial chaos. Francis D'Arcy Cooper, of Cooper Brothers, the firm's auditors, was consulted on matters of policy and joined the board in 1923. It is significant that advice was sought from outside the firm and little reliance was placed on fellow directors. Cooper had the cool and methodical approach of an accountant and became chairman on the death of William Lever in 1925. He had 'the gift of developing a sense of responsibility in subordinates, a quality none too plentiful in a business which for thirty years had been run as a dictatorship'. (For the management problem in running this vast empire, see below, chapter 6.)

William Morris was rather different. Once he had built up Morris Motors in the early 1920s he withdrew more and more from direct management. It became his custom to go on an annual sea voyage to Australia so his managers had to manage. Also Morris did not like formal directors' meetings where he was ill at ease, and preferred to leave the work to his managers provided he was informed of what was going on. The business was never the one-man affair of Lever. Morris attracted some excellent managers such as Miles Thomas and Leonard Lord who were the real managers of the business and were in almost complete control. But there seemed to be some peculiar quirk in his character, hinted at in the various biographies, which made his relationships impermanent. He parted with them all, in different circumstances. He appeared to follow the 'lawn-mower' principle, where any heads which rose above the others were chopped off. There was a mixture of meanness in small things with generosity in large. When he dispensed with anyone the financial treatment was generous, even handsome, in the manner of Catherine the Great with her ex-favourites. In the case of Lord, for example, he was invited to be a trustee of one of Morris's charities which showed there was no personal ill-feeling!

Morris Motors was a one-generation company. It merged with Austin in 1952 to form the British Motor Corporation. Morris became its first chairman but retired after six months and was succeeded by Lord, who had gone to Austin after his dispute with Morris. The two firms were in the managerial stage and eventually fell to Leyland Motors, which was still in the entrepreneurial stage, and which now has the problem of consolidating and managing a variety of businesses which have been taken over.

William Hollins of Nottingham was a textile firm which went back to the Industrial Revolution. It had a steady, good-class trade. One of its best-known trade marks was 'Viyella'. In 1961 Hollins bought the share capital of Gainsborough Cornard, a smaller but expanding company. It also acquired in the process Mr Joe Hyman, a small merchant converter with a family background of textiles and great ambition. He became executive vice-chairman and eventually controlled Hollins. He brought about the change in name to Viyella International.

In the 1960s there was a rapid expansion, largely by acquisitions, and it was generally believed that the old-established textile industry was being revitalised by a strong dose of highly personal and impulsive management. Viyella joined the shares of Rolls Razor and Cyril Lord as those tipped by the pundits to be bought for a glorious investor's future. The business began to run out of steam and many of the proposed mergers, now the only avenue of expansion, broke down.

The management system was highly personal and impulsive. Executives were induced to work hard while they could stand the pace, but there was a large turnover of senior people. In the end the surviving directors called a halt, engineered a palace revolution and Hyman was out.

Second fiddle

One way of providing for continuity is to sell out to a larger organisation, and join that company. But the thrustful entrepreneur either has to rise to the top in the larger organisation (i.e. the latter has bought future management) or he finds life very difficult. It is easier for him to rule in hell than serve in heaven – not that 'heaven' is an apt name for many of the boardroom disputes which have resulted.

John James in fourteen years built up Broadmead to be the largest group of wireless and television shops in the country. He sold the business to the holding company, Firth Cleveland, in 1959 for about £5·8 million, half in cash and half in Firth Cleveland shares, and joined the board. It did not work out and in a short time he left the company. Two thrustful people did not mix. After a brief pause he started out on his own again, looking for a grouping of different businesses, and also joined Williams Supermarkets in the furnishing trade. So far, he has not been able to repeat his early spectacular success.

Kenneth Wood founded the Kenwood kitchen equipment firm, and then sold it to Thorn Electrical Industries in 1968. Thorn's bid was worth about £10 million for the public company, of which Wood's share was £1·2 million. He expected to join the board but at a late stage in the negotiations he was asked to cancel the agreement, resign from the board and accept a consultancy agreement with regard to the Kenwood aspect of Thorn. Shortly after that he re-entered business by joining an old friend in a different line of business.

E. K. Cole founded the Ekco radio manufacturing business in 1922. His company merged with Pye to form British Electronic Industries in 1966, and Cole became deputy chairman. But there were differences of opinion, 'not personal, strictly business disagreements' according to the survivor, and Cole resigned in 1967. In the first year of the amalgamation, the Ekco group had incurred a substantial loss compared with a large profit the previous year, while the Pye group had almost maintained its previous year's profit, so there was obvious scope for disagreement.

In 1962 Bob Tanner and Peter Whitfield had the bright idea of selling membership in hundreds of clubs for one small subscription. They obtained a public quotation in 1967 and then set out, fast. A number of purchases were made; a publicity firm, a collection of betting shops, the manufacturers of amusement machines and language laboratories. They were millionaires on paper only, as the sale of their own shares would have depressed the price. They acquired liquidity by being taken over by Mecca, and exchanged their Clubman's shares for Mecca equity.

Tanner and Whitfield joined the board of Mecca, apparently with a watching brief to look out for promising acquisitions. But they found that they could not do in a large company what they had done for themselves and decided to pull out. They sold all their own shares, about 7 per cent of the Mecca equity, and became 'real' millionaires, and resigned from the company.

Mr Harry Rael-Brook built up a company which was the biggest manufacturer of branded shirts in the country. It was taken over in 1965 by Calico Printers Association for £2·7 million, and he joined the board. But in December 1967 he parted company, 'to go into business on his own'.

Mr Douglas Collins founded Goya perfumes in 1937, as a business specialising in 'inexpensively tiny sizes of expensive perfume', but the major development occurred after the war. In 1960 Reckitt and Son (part of Reckitt and Colman) bought Goya from Collins for about £1½ million. The arrangement did not work too well, he was not the employee type, and part of the business did not fit in with Reckitt's plans, so it was sold back to its founder in 1968 for £800,000. (Certain aspects of the business were retained by Reckitt.)

Similarly Mr Raymond Way, who had started in the used car business in 1932, sold 60 per cent of the business to Kings Motors in 1953 and the remainder in 1959. But the two never properly blended and Way was able to repurchase the business in 1967. The value of the sale in 1953 and 1959 was £650,000 and it was brought back for £400,000.

One step too many

It is evident that business success often comes from one product in a particular market, or the exploitation of a new idea, or of an old one applied in different circumstances. This can create the delusion that the entrepreneur has a magical gift for success and the delusion is fostered by those who tip others to 'back management' and 'back success'. Because a man has been successful in one type of business he jumps to the wholly erroneous conclusion that he can be equally successful in something else, which may require a different technical expertise. Or what is more difficult to detect, the belief that because he has been successful in operating a business on a small scale, largely by his own personal application and control, he can manage a much larger business, which requires an entirely different style of management. As Harrod was told, 'You will go bankrupt unless you learn to keep your coat on', once the business had reached a size in which the owner could no longer serve behind the counter. These business failures are not those which have been weak from the start, but those which have been very successful and then go too far. 'Go softly on lest you come swiftly down, for more men are undone by doing too much trade than doing too little' was Daniel Defoe's advice to the tradesman.[2]

In some cases the one step is a disaster and brings the business down; in others it is not fatal and merely checks the previous expansion. It is fatal where the new development absorbs a large proportion of the firm's activities and there is no slack to take the strain. On the other hand a company with a profitable trade can afford to make a few mistakes, provided they are not too many or too frequent.

Nothing that is said here must give the impression that it is only the ambitious entrepreneur who makes these mistakes. Such mistakes, where serious losses occur, are too obvious to be overlooked. The large multi-product, multi-plant company can make equally serious mistakes, and lose just as much money, but the errors can be glossed over in the annual report and the figures concealed in total accounts. All that happens is that the average rate of profit is reduced by the loss makers. It is a moot point whether some of the spectacular bankruptcies have lost more money for the shareholders as a whole than have some of the large surviving companies who cheerfully drop millions of their own shareholders' money down the drain without the total amount ever being disclosed.

William Lever was no better than anyone else when he went into unfamiliar territory and competed with specialists in other lines. D'Arcy Cooper had to sort out the mess. George Hudson became the Railway King when he consolidated some of the midland railways into a unified system, but overexpansion, and some financial methods and accounting practices which would not satisfy even the rather unexacting requirements of today, brought him down. In the interwar years Gamage, who had built up a good business based on a predominantly men's store in Holborn, plus a country-wide mail order clientele, made the mistake of trying to go into the Oxford Street type of trade with Gamages West End Ltd and failed within two years. As it was a subsidiary company with outside shareholders, much of the loss fell on them and the main business was not brought down in the ruin. Debenhams was built up on the idea of a holding company owning the shares in a large number of good London and provincial drapery shops. The underlying businesses were sound, and many of them still are today, but the pyramiding of debenture and preference capital through holding companies made the organisation vulnerable to a slight fall in trade and profitability and there had to be a financial reorganisation with a severe writing down of capital.

In finance Julian Hodge expanded in twin activities of hire-purchase and merchant banking but overexpansion brought losses and contraction. An Australian, W. R. Wright, built up Pinnock Finance Company largely on the basis of accepting deposits of money from the general public. When the business crashed in 1967 the founder disappeared owing the company £1 million, and 9,000 depositors lost over £9 million. All this is very small change compared with the operations of Bernie Cornfeld in America, and later in the rest of the world. He was a superb salesman, and could teach other people to sell. He used the basic principle of the mutual fund (in England the unit trust) whereby people are induced to invest their savings in the various 'funds' and this pooled money is invested for them. In the stricter form, the money is invested in marketable securities and a management fee is collected. Of course the return on the investment is dependent on the underlying profitability of the shares in which the money is invested. Much is made of the professional investment skill of the managers, but on average there is little to prove that this really exists. In its less respectable form the money may be used for speculative ventures. When one or two of these come off the illusion of invincibility is created and money pours in, proving that Barnum underestimated human gullibility and that at least two are born every minute!

Cornfeld discovered that there were thousands of Americans throughout the world, servicemen, administrators of aid programmes, oil men, etc., who were rich in local currency but with little to spend the money on. High-pressure salesmanship on commission, which made an encyclopedia salesman look like a sleepy village storekeeper, brought in a vast flow of money. Operations were extended to many countries, and often local currency was siphoned off, contrary to local exchange controls, into American investments. His Investors Overseas Services was banned from operations in many countries, including the United States, and any of its citizens anywhere. When some of the investments failed to be profitable and people wanted their money back there was a liquidity crisis and Cornfeld was voted off the board, although he later returned. The bubble burst in 1970 and affairs are still being sorted out.

Robert Maxwell went into the rather staider activity of publishing. He concentrated mainly on scientific and technical publications (there is always a demand for back numbers of important articles, and they have their price) and on combining together encyclopedia firms. He was tipped for greatness – when he made a bid for Butterworth's, John Davis, in the *Observer* of 15 October 1967, commented:

> On Maxwell's record it is hard to disagree. Not only have Pergamon shares risen from 15*s.* 11*d.* to 39*s.* 7½*d.* since they were marketed in 1964, but Maxwell has displayed throughout his rise a remarkable administrative flair, which has enabled him to squeeze quart-sized profits out of some unimaginative pint pots.

But when the proposed amalgamation with the American firm Leasco fell through because of disputes regarding the profit figures and other matters, a Department of Trade and Industry inquiry was set up, which produced an interim report in July 1971, severely critical of many aspects of industry and finance. The evidence is disputed by many of the people concerned, but the point at issue here is that another bubble had burst.

Charles Clore, largely through bids and takeovers through Sears Holdings, built up a vast industrial empire and a great reputation in the 1950s. The mere mention of his name in connection with a company would cause the share price to rise and the financial experts to become lyrical. Since then, while there has been no failure of the kind that some other companies have suffered, the magic has gone and ordinary human mortality is detected. Sears Holdings is no longer a glamour stock, there is nothing outstanding about its return on capital; the acquisitions are a miscellaneous collection of companies, none of which is outstanding in its own trade; the venture into shipping, British Oil Shipping, vanished into a stake in Anglo-Norness, which also had its difficulties; but the biggest of all the burst bubbles was City Centre. Three postwar entrepreneurs, Walter Flack, Jack Cotton and Charles Clore, each rode the postwar property boom. In 1960 they amalgamated and:[3]

> The marriage of Cotton, Clore and Flack in 1960 was one of the most ill fated corporate marriages ever. Clore found out that Cotton had virtually no organisation at all. An accountant, a couple of typists, and perhaps half a dozen clerks. The boardroom of City Centre was Cotton's suite at the Dorchester. In his bedroom were two beds, one was spread with the files which only he could touch.

Three strong-willed men who were each accustomed to having their way produced three-sided boardroom battles and an atmosphere of bitterness.

Market changes

Businesses on the way up thrive under the right market conditions. When these change, successful businesses can run into difficulties. This, however, is not the whole explanation. Some of the outstanding achievements have been in areas where the market conditions were created by the entrepreneur; others have been in old-established industries, slow and sluggish, which have been given a new lease of life by a different personality, and it is only after the success that the opportunities appear to have been so obvious. Similarly, when market conditions become adverse it is the function of the entrepreneur to recognise the changed circumstances and to change accordingly. Yet it is often difficult for this adaptation to take place. Generals skilled on the offensive are not always adept at fighting rearguard actions. One of the major difficulties is to recognise and distinguish between what may be a temporary setback and what may be a long-term decline in the fortunes of the industry.

For example, the development of road transport in the interwar years made inevitable cuts in the quantity of rail travel. Companies had to make adjustments. Falling revenue in such cases is no evidence of lack of ability or even of the spirit of enterprise. A willingness to meet the competition with new ideas and developments could reduce the fall in profits. Even to make profits at all in difficult circumstances may show considerably more business ability than to make large profits in very easy times. Then, the railway companies brought down their expenses in line with the fall in revenue, even if they were unable to cut them to the same extent.

Colliery companies, faced with the competition of oil, may successfully reduce their extraction costs by new methods; there is nothing they can do to offset the exhaustion of the coal seams. After the wartime expansion in engineering and munitions the iron and steel industry from the 1920s to the 1930s faced the 'black decade' when no profits were earned. Again, the decline in the overseas market for cheap cotton goods brought an inevitable contraction in the industry. Sometimes in the endeavour to counteract the decline in a market, mistaken decisions are taken which make matters worse.

Just as the entrepreneur who is carried on by the flood tide of an expanding market attracts an unmerited adulation, so the businessman struggling in the fell clutch of circumstance attracts a host of unknowledgeable critics and a crop of peculiar remedies. These mostly involve some kind of reorganisation of the industry, the amalgamation of different businesses, and the almost meaningless use of the word 'rationalisation' to cover many quite irrational ideas, when the basic fact is that there must be some contraction in the industry.

A toy case study

The ups and downs of the business world can be seen in microcosm in the toy industry, which illustrates many of the points that have been discussed above.

Meccano was a 'two-generation' set-up. At the beginning of the century Frank Hornby, with the assistance of his two sons, cut up copper sheeting, bored holes and started the Meccano construction kits that fathers found difficulty in allowing their sons to play with at all. The beauty of the idea was that the kit could be built up with successive Christmas presents to a complete outfit. Hornby trains followed, with their own built-in possibilities of extension, and Dinky toys in the postwar years. In 1956 profits approached £1 million.

But in 1964 the Meccano company ended its independent existence 'in a sour, unhappy mess of mounting losses, angry shareholders, and un-met forecasts'.[4] The chairman, Roland Hornby, the son of the founder, blamed it all on the trains. Modern houses were too small, and parents were spending the money on cars, washing machines and hire-purchase. Much of the railway equipment had to be severely written down. Hornby, the pioneers, found that many other people climbed on their band-wagon, but the main cause of the disaster was that their rivals had their own band-wagons to mount. It was not the case that other companies imitated their products, they made them obsolete. Dinky toys had had the market to itself, but Ullman and Katz with the Mettoy company brought out cars like the real thing, with opening doors, real windows and independent suspension on their 'Corgi' range, and Smith and Odell of Lesney Products brought out their 'Matchbox' scale model toys at a third of the price of Dinky.

Meccano was still Meccano, but there were many other types of construction kits on the market, and Hornby's claim that Meccano was 'a magical name' is reminiscent of that real motor car with 'the magic of a name'. The company was slow to accept new ideas and was taken over by Lines Brothers in 1964.

Lines Brothers was formed in 1919 and became a public company in 1933. The three brothers gave the name Tri-ang(le) to their products. Like Hornby it is in the second generation. It makes toys, baby carriages, etc., and at the time of the takeover it, too, had suffered a decline in profit from the previous year, and was undergoing a considerable reorganisation, closing uneconomic factories, reducing capital expenditure and cutting out unprofitable products.

As recently as 1968 Lesney Products, the makers of 'Matchbox' toys, which was founded just after the war, was one of the glamour stocks in the country. Its market capitalisation (i.e. the stock exchange value of the shares times the number of shares) was roughly a third of British Leyland. Mettoy, the other diecast model maker, enjoyed a similar status. Within three years the position had changed completely. Much of the postwar expansion had been in overseas markets, especially in the USA and Canada. Other makers were catching up and an American company, Mattel, made the technical advance of low friction wheels and plastic tracks. In 1971 Mettoy experienced large redundancies and Lesney closed factories.

The Lines reorganisation did not halt the fall in profits and the shareholders pressed for action. Consultants were brought in and seven directors resigned, including four members of the Lines family. Only one remained, as chairman of the company. A new managing director was brought in from outside and other experienced executives were appointed. There were extensive factory closures and about a third of the production units were cut back and the labour force reduced from 10,500 to 8,500. The number of soft toys was reduced from 180 to 90. A tough system of budgetary control was introduced.[5]

But time and money were against the company, which needed an influx of capital and several years before recovery could take place, and the company went into voluntary liquidation at the end of 1971. All the major companies were in difficulties, including the American. The market had suffered from overexpansion in the postwar period and there was too much potential production. The market was becoming increasingly volatile and changeable, as children who accepted space travel as a normal part of life were not content with static toys. They were alleged to be maturing earlier and were switching from toys to pop records. But catastrophies can overwhelm old-established 'managed' companies as well as young forceful ones.

Notes

1 Napoleon's empire was a one-generation firm. Later attempts to revive it under a nephew were unsuccessful in face of foreign competition.
2 Daniel Defoe, *The Complete English Tradesman.*
3 Oliver Marriott, *The Property Boom,* Hamish Hamilton, 1967.
4 Peter Wilsher, 'Derailment on the nursery floor', *Sunday Times,* 16 February 1964.
5 'Operation bootstrap', *Financial Times,* 18 June 1971.

Four

The board of directors

> The directors of such companies are managers of other people's money rather than of their own.
>
> Adam Smith, *Wealth of Nations*

The businessmen we are considering, whether entrepreneurs or managers, almost invariably operate through the institution of the joint-stock company. This excludes for the moment consideration of economic activities carried out by public boards, local authorities and other forms. The joint-stock company as the normal method of conducting business has been universally accepted, although its acceptance in the last century was neither immediate nor ungrudging.

The basic theory behind the joint-stock company is corporate status and, while not essential but usual in practice, the limited liability of the members of the company. Originally the company form was used to facilitate the employment of a very large amount of capital on some enterprise which was beyond the financial resources of one man or a partnership, or to engage in ventures which were particularly risky and in which merchants were willing to venture a part only of their capital. So the obvious scope for companies was in overseas trade where the returns were slow and uncertain, and in such undertakings as canals, waterworks and railways. People subscribed for shares in these companies and made either a profitable or an unprofitable investment, but in the latter case their loss was limited to the amount that they had invested. No further loss fell on them, unlike the sole trader or partnership where each man was liable to his creditors to 'his last shilling and last acre'. Now, under the Companies Acts, anyone can separate his business life from his personal life by registering his business as a company. The company may fail and be wound up but the shareholder incurs no personal bankruptcy. He 'may lose everything except honour' and what he has had the forethought to put in his wife's name. It is possible to buy a company ready made for a few pounds and acquire the status of a company director.

Early companies, such as canal and railway companies, were formed by a few knowledgeable people, landowners, bankers, mine owners and industrialists because they could see the direct beneficial effect on their own activities. The shareholders were few in number with a large financial interest. They could keep a close watch on those elected as directors. The later companies, the conversions of the family businesses from the middle of the nineteenth century, had a similar share structure. Even after converting to public companies the ownership and control tended to be in few hands. The directors were substantial shareholders; Lever and Morris held all the ordinary shares in their companies and the general public could buy only preference shares.

Today the very large companies, such as ICI, Shell or Unilever, have thousands of shareholders, each with a comparatively moderate holding in the company, moderate in relation to the total capital and often moderate in total amount. It is therefore impossible for the shareholders to know the directors personally, or to meet as a body at the annual meeting, unless Wembley Stadium is hired for the purpose! Moreover, the wise policy for the outside investor without direct control is to spread the risk, so that a comparatively affluent shareholder will spread his investments over a number of different companies, relying on the profitability of his portfolio as a whole rather than on the success of any particular investment. If one turns out badly he may sigh but can do little else. (The position of the 'institutional investor' will be dealt with below.)

There is a negative sense in which it may be said that the shareholders tacitly elect the directors. When a company comes before the public for the first time by the issue of a prospectus and the investor decides to subscribe to the shares, by supporting the company he is presumably supporting the directors who are in control of the company; and the shareholder who buys existing shares through the stock exchange can hardly complain about the present management. If he remains a shareholder without directly voting for the directors he is accepting them in the sense that a citizen accepts the government of his country if he does not 'vote with his feet' and emigrate. The alternative in both cases can be expensive. The shareholder who sells out when the company runs into difficulties is liable to sell at a loss; what would be better would be a revival in the fortunes of his company by some means, but there is little he can do about this. But this little does not mean that he is powerless, and there are times, such as the threat of a takeover or the occasion of boardroom dissension, when he exercises the ultimate power and is courted like a beauty queen. There have been a number of occasions since the war where the votes of the small shareholders have been unexpectedly decisive in accepting or rejecting outside bids. Powerful boards have been defeated. This is little different from political democracy where the ordinary man in the street who has normally to be guided by his betters is, every five years, suddenly transformed into an intelligent voter. When there is a vacancy on the board, the shareholders cannot meet and discuss the virtues of a possible candidate. The matter is decided by the board, or the chairman, and someone is invited to take the vacant place. This of course has to be confirmed by the shareholders at the next meeting, after the chairman has extolled the virtues of the member he has been fortunate enough to have discovered, even if the search went no farther than his own son.

Thus 'shareholders' democracy' in practice is the rule of the few and not of the many, and boards of directors have been aptly described as self-perpetuating oligarchies, being elected and re-elected by themselves and their immediate supporters. The management of large companies is in the hands of people who in many cases may have little or no direct financial interest in the company. But the position of the directors, especially in more recent times, is not as strong as it might appear. As in political oligarchies there may be internal struggles for power and succession, and there may be invasion from competing oligarchies or even, in rare instances, a peasants' revolt. Even a large personal shareholding may be no insurance against revolt and enforced exile.

The functions of the board

The board has to direct the affairs of the company in the interests of the owners of the company, and is in the position of being a trustee of others' property. Strictly speaking, the board is not concerned with management, but has the task of appointing and controlling the managers. This distinction is blurred in practice in Britain, but in German law there is the two-tier board in which the board proper may be representative of various interests and it supervises the lower board which performs the direct management functions. No member of the board, as such, exercises any particular function. He is a member of a committee which has a collective responsibility The innocent will immediately say that this is all wrong, because boards have Works Directors, Sales Directors, etc. (we are now into capital letters), so the board members do have particular functions.

But all this means is that the man is exercising two functions; in one he is an executive of the company, carrying out the general instructions of the board and in the other he has an overall responsibility for the total conduct of the company. It is no good speaking up vehemently when his own interests are questioned, and dozing off when decisions are taken which involve the company in great financial difficulties, on the excuse that it was not his responsibility.

It is usual to concentrate the management through one, or more, general managers, appointed and instructed by the board. Again, he may be, and in practice usually is, a member of the board, and in this case he is the managing director. But again it must be most strongly emphasised that a managing director is exercising two separate and distinct functions: he is acting as a director of the company with the same responsibility as the other directors, and he is acting as a general manager, responsible to the very board of which he is an important member. The tasks, qualities and responsibilities are quite distinct and there may be cases in which a conflict of interests and responsibilities takes place.

When the board meets it must have a chairman, who could be elected for the occasion, but it is usual to have a permanent chairman, who also takes the chair at annual meetings of the shareholders. (The Athenian democratic principle of treating all as equals and rotating the office among the members of the board is not adopted.) Again, the function of the chairman is to take the chair at the various meetings, he is a director among others. However, he is obviously a senior and influential member of the board, unless he is some figurehead introduced to confer tone to the proceedings. Whether he is senior or inferior to the managing director is largely a question of where the power lies within the company. In some companies the offices of chairman and 'chief executive' are combined, which solves the problem of conflict by dispensing with the check and balance inherent in the normal constitution.

That is the general theory. In practice the board structure depends largely on the historical development of the company and the strength of the various members of the board. It is unusual for the company to spring fully armed from the companies registration department and to start business on a large scale, such as the nineteenth-century railway companies (although their godlike paternity was the Act of Parliament), and most companies have grown from small beginnings. Thus the steps are, small business of a sole trader or partnership (normally registered as a company for reasons given above); expansion to a larger company; conversion to a public company with a public issue or sale of shares; and if fortunate, growth to a very large company. It is the latter with which we are mainly concerned.

Thus at the early stages the one man (or two or three) is the principal shareholder, the driving force, the managing director and chairman. Even on conversion to a company with outside participation in the ownership, it is the founder or his successor who is the principal shareholder and chief executive. As we have seen above, the control may still be in the hands of the founding family even at a very large size – or the ownership and control may be diffused among a larger number of people. But the problems of establishing and developing a new business are different from operating a mature business. Different techniques and approaches may be necessary, and these may require different men to operate them. This watershed in the company's affairs may give rise to personal clashes. Another cause of dispute may occur when the external circumstances change, such as the saturation of a once profitable market or the rise of new competition. Again, the defensive techniques, and the generals, will have to be different. The self-perpetuating oligarchy is much less secure than might appear at first sight.

In 1970, when Lines Brothers first ran into difficulties, seven directors left the board, including four out of five of the family members, one of whom was the eighty-eight-year-old chairman, one of the founders. Most of the ex-directors remained as executives of the company as they had service contracts. In 1971 Sir David Brown was forced by bankers' pressure to take a less active part in the management of the David Brown Corporation which he had founded (*Daily Telegraph*, 1 July 1971). In the same year the chairman of Star (GB) Holdings, one of the large property groups, resigned over differences of opinion with the other directors. 'The difference arose because Mr Potel pushed for further expansion while the rest of the board wanted a period of consolidation following the mergers and acquisitions of the past two years' (*Financial Times*, 12 June 1971). It was announced that he would continue to be associated with Star in 'a non-executive consultancy capacity'. The new chief executive was a man who had joined the company when his own company was taken over in 1968 – a story which is repeated many times! We have seen other examples of founders, such as Selfridge and Lipton, who were displaced when the companies ran into difficulties, with or without the honorary presidency.

Takeovers

One of the obvious opportunities for disputes occurs after a take-over, especially where the new management believes that it can manage the acquisition better than its former directors. From the point of view of those taken over, it does not appear to matter whether the merger was 'friendly' or not. The willing victims can delay, but not avert, the fall of the chopper. The exceptional cases are where the man taken over is influential enough because of shareholding, or because of personal ability, or preferably both, to rise to the top in the new circumstances.

Leyland Motors acquired control of Standard-Triumph in May 1961 through a share exchange. The chairman of Leyland, Sir Henry Spurrier, became chairman of Standard. In August of the same year without any warning he got rid of all but one of the Standard directors, including Mr Alick Dick, an international figure in the industry. The formula in these cases is that the directors are asked to tender their resignations. Some were retained in executive posts. Spurrier's successor, Lord Stokes, repeated the process when Leyland took over BMC, although the bloodshed was not immediate. But it did not occur with the two smaller and specialist companies, Rover and Jaguar.

Clore acquired Lewis Investment Trust in 1965. His first task was to improve the position of Selfridges, which had been acquired previously by Lewis's. By 1969 the group was ready to deal with the main part of Lewis's. The managing director and his assistant, who had been with the firm since 1930, were suddenly asked to resign. As one employee stated, 'After the shake-up at Selfridges we knew it was only a matter of time before it happened to us' (*Financial Times*, 28 March 1969).

Coats Paton took over the Jaeger clothing firm in 1965 but it was not until 1969 that the managing director, a son of the former chairman, and the finance director both resigned. After a long silence which created an illusion of contentment following the merger of Calico Printers with English Sewing Cotton, Sir John Barlow announced that he was leaving the board because of a policy disagreement. The chairman was reported to have uttered the anguished cry: 'We just expected him to say he was retiring' (*Financial Times*, 14 August 1968). When GEC took over AEI after a long and contested battle, none of the directors survived for long although a few joined GEC in the early stages. Sir Frank Schon, a refugee from the Nazis in 1939, built up Marchon Products, which was merged with Albright and Wilson in 1956. He became a director, but retired in 1967 owing to differences about company policy.

It does not require a takeover or the ousting of an aged founder to provide the conditions for boardroom dissensions. Wm McIlroy, the Reading department store, was founded in 1875, and in 1945 the son of the founder converted it into a public company to provide for succession. The business had always been a middle-class drapery business, but the new management, according to the vendor, attempted to turn it into an ultra-fashionable store, and its profitability declined. The conflicting statements, the adjournment of the annual meeting, and the attempts at mediation all enlivened the financial Press in 1950.

Wall Paper Manufacturers is an almost classic case of the family business merger. It was formed in 1889 during a trade depression by the merger of eighteen family businesses, and later ten others were drawn in; in fact when competition developed, the usual policy was to try to buy it out. Although the proportional financial interests of the founding families declined, the influence did not. In the 1960s most of the directors were sons or grandsons of the founders, but the business never became a closely knit, unified organisation. In 1960 a new chairman was brought in and he tried to centralise and rationalise the diverse group. There was strong disagreement as to the solution to the company's troubles, which amounted to a virtually static trade in an expanding market, with other companies such as ICI cutting into the trade with its new emulsion paint while WPM stuck to distemper. Matters came to a head when the chairman was abroad on company business. His vice-chairman informed him that there was trouble. He returned. The chairman and vice-chairman were outvoted nine to two and both subsequently resigned. (There is the warning from Richard I, 'Never go on a Crusade and leave malcontents behind.')

The plum, if that is the right metaphor for a company with its record and problems, was ripe for the picking. After an abortive joint attempt by Courtaulds and Reed Paper, the latter acquired control in 1965.

The blow may be sudden. Mr Cecil King, the chairman of the International Publishing Corporation, who had been a member of the staff for forty-two years, a member of the board for thirty-nine years, and chairman for seventeen years, received a letter from the secretary of the company at 8.15 on 30 May 1968, when he was shaving, asking him to resign – quietly.

One of the fiercer rows was the 1965 dispute at British Printing Corporation. This was the aftermath of the merger between the Purnell group, which incorporated a number of famous printing firms, and the Hazell–Sun group, in 1964. The *News of the World* organisation had made a bid for Hazell–Sun. To prevent this, Hazell–Sun's chairman, Lord Crowther, approached Purnell's chairman, Mr Wilfred Harvey, who had been mainly responsible for building it from a small local printing works to its present size for a merger. This took the form of Purnell borrowing £5 million to outbid the *News of the World*. It was a wedding concluded in haste, the shotgun in this case being brandished by an unwelcome suitor, and there appeared to be serious differences of opinion as to the actual arrangement that was made. Hazell–Sun thought it was a marriage of equals, particularly as it was agreed that the new board of the British Printing Corporation was to contain four directors from each side with Harvey as chairman. Hazell–Sun directors complained that there was a long delay in setting up the new board and that certain information was withheld from them. Purnell's attitude appeared to be that it had taken over Hazell–Sun, and that Purnell arrangements were nothing to do with the satellite.

When in 1965 the Hazell–Sun directors finally got a sight of the Purnell directors' service agreements the storm broke. Harvey was entitled to a commission on the gross profits *before* interest. This automatically raised the commission due as it included the Hazell–Sun profit in the group, but took no account of the cost of the money borrowed to bring about the amalgamation. It was also a matter of dispute that new agreements had been made just before the amalgamation took place. The main complaint was of non-disclosure. There was also objection to the appointment of two new directors, connected with Purnell, at a meeting called at such short notice that it had been impossible for all the directors to attend. This of course disturbed the balance of power. After threatening to call an extraordinary meeting of the company, the dispute was finally settled by Mr Harvey's resignation.

The merger between Trust Houses and Forte in 1970 had a similar outcome. There were deep dissensions between the two sides on the new board, which led to a takeover bid for the company by Allied Breweries. This was foiled mainly because of the large personal holding of Sir Charles Forte. In 1966 there were disputes in Berger Jenson and Nicholson (Magicote paint) and the chairman was replaced by the vice-chairman when the former proposed that he retire in favour of an outside chairman. The row was eventually settled by the appointment of an outside chairman. The managing director of Fisons resigned in 1962 because of 'serious and prolonged differences with the chairman'; it was said of one former chairman of International Computers (a merger of various interests) that his success lay in his ability, no doubt gained in the civil service, to placate the various factions within ICT which were seeking power; and the bitter and controversial boardroom dispute at Pye ended in an out-of-court settlement with substantial compensation for the former managing director. There were open disputes in Brough Nicholson and Hall in 1963, resulting in damages for wrongful dismissal; two family members of the board of J. Bibby and Sons resigned on family differences in 1967; the chairman of Gas Purification resigned in 1961 following a dispute; the managing director of Inveresk Paper was replaced by the finance director, and when the latter was asked if the former holder resigned or was sacked, stated, 'Let's just say he relinquished his position as a result of some internal changes and I'm picking up the reins.' It could not be more nicely put! Sir Joseph Causton and Sons suffered bitter boardroom politics for three years, with a regular series of resignations; the Ross family lost control of Ross Group, and the meetings of the Bear Brand hosiery company provided journalists with lively and interesting copy.

It is certainly tough at the top, whether the occupants of the position are founder members, people taken over, those doing the taking over, or bright boys brought in to revitalise a company.

Composition of the board

As we have seen above, the composition of the board of the new, small or growing company largely settles itself. The board is the owner, founder or driver, assisted and surrounded by a number of his appointees, or in some cases of members brought in to represent some other interest, such as financial backing given to the company. The problem we have here is what sort of board should manage the affairs of a mature, large and old-established company?

One problem is that of technical expertise. If one reads many of the books on specialised aspects of business or management, such as purchasing, sales, production, transport, etc., one will find that the authors, in explaining the importance of their particular function and its place in the organisation, perhaps with the help of a rudimentary organisation chart, will claim that this function must be represented at board level. One cannot blame them for pushing the great importance in the scheme of things of the skills and expertise which they have made their life work and absorbing interest – that is the function of a trade union anywhere, to push the interests of its members – but one must also recognise that this is special pleading.

But a board which directly catered for all interests which are important in the operation of the company would be very large indeed. It is generally recognised that any deliberative body which has to come to some sort of executive decision is ineffective if too large. As has been said of committees, and a board of directors is really a committee of the shareholders of the company, the ideal number of members is three, one who knows what he is doing, one deaf and the third absent. Twenty or thirty people cannot take business decisions, with all the members participating in the discussion; the meetings would drag on and on. Some few people take the decisions and the rest agree.

So, some of the functions cannot be represented directly at board level, but lower down in some sort of management grouping – for example, a sales director will be responsible for home sales, overseas sales, advertising, market research, etc. Or if preferred, he can be given the title of marketing director, but he is still concerned with the sale of the company's products. The production director is responsible for the production departments, internal works transport, manpower allocation, development, etc. It is not necessary that the heads of all these departments and sub-departments are on the board deliberating over the general issues of the company.

Btu objections have been made to even this lesser form of

representation at the top. The argument runs that the board is dealing with the company as a whole and is not an internal representative body of often competing interests. These interests are managerial and are to be dealt with by the people who are appointed for their ability as managers, and who may or may not have the qualities required in a director. In fact they may be all the better as managers and as technical experts if they do not have the characteristics of the director. It is the function and duty of the experts to put their case to the board, but just as war is too important to be left to the generals, so is company direction quite different from skilled management.

The danger here is that the expert has too much influence and may devote it all to the furtherance of his own speciality. He is less willing to view the firm as a whole, and is usually incapable of making the mental adjustment from the application of specialised knowledge to that of viewing the operations of the business as an integrated whole. An inability to understand simple financial matters is one cause for complaint. Another danger is that the expert will expect to be left alone to carry out his own function and therefore will not query the proposals of other experts – dog does not eat dog. In a large multi-product organisation, where the heads of divisional boards sit on the main board and where there may be rivalry between them for a share in the firm's capital expenditure budget, the gentlemanly approach is still 'I will not oppose your project if you do not oppose mine'. Where the chairman or managing director is the chief figure on the subsidiary board its decisions are even less likely to be questioned by other directors on the main board. This was the case with AEI when Lord Chandos was chairman of the company and of the group boards.[1]

When J. Bibby and Sons engaged in a reorganisation in 1967 because of poor profitability the chairman stated (*Sunday Times*, 21 May 1967):

> I had felt for some time that the board was unduly weighted with full time executives and this tended to make it a management committee too ingrown in its attitudes and too lacking in knowledge of the outside business world for our present and future needs.

Bibby's was a classic case of a production-minded company, with a wide spread of products. There were many others. One chairman of GEC had to have a 'rights issue' of capital explained to him;

other chairmen cannot understand why there is a shortage of capital when the company is stuffed with reserves on the liabilities side of the balance sheet. In the postwar period the big three electrical companies were renowned for the excellence of their products and the skill of their engineers – and a decline in their profitability. They were 'production conscious' on the heavy engineering side. Lord Hirst of GEC, who looked at the market first and took the advice of his technical experts, was looked down on by the engineers as being a mere salesman. Metropolitan-Vickers, one of the constituent firms of AEI, had an excellent technical record but poor profits; the official history of the company barely mentions profits, and twenty-one years after the amalgamation there is hardly a mention in the history of M-V of the parent company AEI. The attitude was typified by an M-V spokesman who complained of the City's trying to check his expenditure of 'so-called shareholders' money'.

Cunard went deeper into trouble and delayed reform because of technical influence at the top; in this case the traditional emphasis on large passenger liners which were losing money heavily and dragging down the profitable side of the business. It was said that the Rolls-Royce management, very much an engineer-dominated company, was more perturbed by the technical failure of carbon fibre blades for the RB 211 than they were by the mounting costs and unprofitability of their operations.

This is the danger of the purely 'technical' board which does not recognise that whatever the product, and however interesting and fascinating the technical problems, the company is in business. At the worst it must cover its costs in order to survive. Better still it should have a profit record which prevents its being taken over by an entrepreneur who will wield the hatchet and cause a massacre of its technological innocents.

The outside director

One remedy for this inbreeding and lack of balance is the purely non-executive board. The board directs and management is in the hands of a general manager. Banks and insurance companies tend towards this structure. The prewar railway companies drew their directors from a very wide field, taking in finance, major customers, the peerage and the services. This is exceptional, if only because historically most companies have owed, and many still owe, a great deal to the entrepreneurial qualities and family inheritance of certain individuals.

The compromise is to have a board made up primarily of career executives plus a leavening of 'outsiders'. This may vary from bringing in one man as chairman with the personal qualities of a diplomat and a World Cup referee on a full-time basis, to a larger number of people, full- or part-time, to represent various qualities and experience, such as a representative of the company's merchant bankers for financial advice, somebody from an allied industry such as a main supplier or customer, or a director who is 'a specialist' in general ideas. In the larger public company many of these directors are national figures.

This can be seen clearly in ICI where the policy is clearly explained in several of its annual reports. Most of the directors are career men who came to the company as chemists or engineers and have come up through the ranks – the commissioned ranks of course. When on the board, although responsible for a particular line or staff function, these functions bear no direct relationship to their particular expertise, i.e. a chemist may have overall supervision of a group of activities, say fertilisers and explosives, *and* overall responsibility for a staff function, such as personnel. The immediate reaction is that no man can be responsible for such large and diverse functions, but the merit is that as he cannot manage in detail he is forced to delegate the details of operations to his subsidiary boards or functional managers, and is exercising the true functions of a director in being just that, a director and not a manager.

The five or six non-executive directors have no specific function but they bring in outside experience. (The company got one chairman from this source: Sir Paul Chambers joined the company at the top from the Inland Revenue, and was eventually elected chairman.) One of their functions is to view the proposals of the experts. They form an internal court of appeal. Ideas put forward not only have to convince other technical experts but the outsiders – a sort of quorum of devil's advocates. Another is to agree the salaries of the executive directors. Company directors and members of Parliament are two bodies who fix their own salaries.

It has been suggested that this policy should be extended to all companies; that the duties of non-executive directors be redefined specifically as supervisors of the day-to-day managers; that there should be a minimum number of them on the board; and that they are required to report to the shareholders.[2]

This idea is attractive. The contrast is often made between the normal British practice of executive boards with the American one of having a larger proportion of non-executive directors – and too many people are of the opinion that if the British practice differs from the American the British is, by definition, necessarily wrong. While we see the disadvantages of our system, the Americans too are criticising the operations of their own, such as the failure of non-executive directors to prevent the collapse of companies, and the conflict of interest where directors have access to company information in merger possibilities. While the presence of good, active and powerful outside directors might have prevented some of the spectacular losses of the 'technical' boards, there are others where this is not the case. Equally, there are the successful companies with fully executive boards.

For example, AEI had a large number of non-executive directors but they were never able to make AEI a unified organisation and it eventually fell to GEC. Even their outside experience could not make the company profit-conscious. At one time or another John Bloom had a variety of experienced and successful people on the board of Rolls Razor but this did not forestall bankruptcy.

It does very much depend on what the outside director is expected to do. At one extreme he need be little more than window-dressing – the company acquires a well-known man or title and the director acquires a free lunch or a guinea or two for attendance. It is an old story. 'The readiness with which gentlemen, or respectability, wealth, and intelligence, allow their names to be attached to companies, with whose principles they are but little acquainted, is much to be regretted', wrote Charles Babbage in 1826.[3] The term 'guinea-pig' director came into use about the same time. Even in 1970 one company chairman stated that his reason for appointing such men was to 'create public confidence in the company's image'. The low fees paid, in about half the cases in a 1970 survey under £1,000 a year, less than that paid to a manual worker, is a measure of the company's evaluation of his contribution. (A large number of such directorships, small in themselves, can build up into a most useful source of income.)

It is no consolation to an investor who loses his money to find that certain distinguished names were on the board of the company, especially if they managed to get into the lifeboat before the ship went down.

At the other extreme is the man who is eagerly sought after because he has a great deal to contribute. In fact an outsider, not hidebound in the company's traditions, or committed to a particular technical expertise, can come in at the top and in this way chair several companies at the same time. There is no reason why an outsider in this sense should not be full time, with purely directorial functions and without concern for the day-to-day management. But truly able men such as these are scarce.

In between there are many gradations. One can see the value of an expert joining a board for his particular expertise such as D'Arcy Cooper as auditor to Unilever, or Sir Paul Chambers as finance expert to ICI. Experts can plug a leaky hole in the company's organisation. Others probably contribute little. Even if they are directors of other companies with technical expertise, it does not follow that the individual director (who relies on *his* experts) brings this knowledge to the new company.

From first principles it is difficult to see what contribution can be made. If there are a dozen or more directors and the board meets once a month, and there are a number of items to be discussed, there is not the time for any really deep discussion of important problems, especially if the chairman has a train to catch. The director can nod wisely at the right time or ask a simple question.

It would appear that the main contribution the outside director can make is wisdom. The standard phrase used by a company chairman when a director dies, retires, or is eased out of office is 'We shall miss his wise counsel'. In many cases where a fundamental error has been the cause of large losses, it is remarkable that the board contained experts whose function was to look to these matters.

Directors' shares

As the directors form a committee of shareholders it might be expected that a first qualification is that they are shareholders in the company. Most companies recognise this by having a minimum number of qualifying shares to be held by each director. But in the case of many very large companies this shareholding is ridiculously small, both in relation to the total capital and in relation to the income and status of the director. If, say, the minimum holding is 500 shares, with a market value of £2 each, this is an investment in the company of £1,000, for a man whose salary and fees from his position may be anything above £10,000 a year.

Even this is sometimes considered too large. A few years ago, one of the largest companies in this country proposed a sharp reduction in the number of qualifying shares on the grounds that it was difficult to promote people to the board if they had to find several hundreds or thousands of pounds to put down to buy shares in the company. If a man has risen up through the company, and has enjoyed a high salary as an executive, and in his forties or fifties has not accumulated sufficient personal capital to invest in his own company on promotion to the board, he does not seem to have managed his own finances well enough to qualify him to be a manager of other people's money. Or, if his bank manager would not be prepared to make the necessary advance on his prospects, he ought to change his bank.

Where a director holds a very small number of shares, his interest in the company is that of a manager or an employee. His income depends on his director's fees and service contract, and not on the dividends received out of the profits; in fact, with surtax on the unearned dividends the latter can mean less to him than the use of a company car or the directors' lunch. It will require a great effort of will to think of the outside shareholders' interests. Where the personal holding is very large, dividends and the maintenance of the capital value of the shareholding is important to the director, as a shareholder. In some takeovers, where the vendor's large personal holding is bought out in shares of the acquiring company, he ends up by being among the largest private holders, dwarfing the holdings of the employee holders who have taken him over. Sir Arnold Weinstock in GEC and the Showering brothers in Allied Breweries are two examples of this.

Yet there are always exceptions. There are large public companies where the family holdings are very large indeed, often in the second or third generation, where the reputation for dynamism and for the development of the company is very low. Where hundreds of thousands, or even millions of pounds are at stake, better results should be expected. Perhaps the cushion of inherited wealth is so large that no particular exertion is required? Even so, with these cases, there is much to be said for the structure of industry where the directors personally lose money if the company fails, and do not continue to ride round in their carriages splashing the people they have ruined.

The institutional shareholder

So far we have been talking about the owners as individuals. But a large, and increasing, proportion of the capital of companies is in the hands of various institutions. Pension funds and life assurance companies are collecting large sums of money now against an obligation to pay out future benefits. The money may be invested traditionally in government stock, property and land, or in equity capital. While the proportions change from time to time, vast sums have gone into ordinary shares, so the major insurance companies and pension funds are very significant shareholders in large public companies.

These investors are not the traditional widows and orphans so beloved of company law reformers, whose ignorance leaves them prey to the unscrupulous. They are professional specialised managerial experts in investment. The innocent in these affairs might therefore expect that the members of the boards of companies would be looking nervously over their shoulders at, say, an insurance company which holds a large block of shares, or at a group of such companies which between them control perhaps one-third of the votes. The boards have little need to worry. On the whole the institutional investor, in spite of his alleged expertise, exercises no more control than the widow living in retirement at Bournemouth.

The reasons given for this lack of intervention are twofold. With such huge sums for investment the funds rapidly run out of investment opportunities if they confine their activities to a few leading companies, or else they would end up by being the sole shareholder. They have to find more and more companies. The result is that the major institutions have large and varied portfolios, on the sound investment principle of not having all their eggs in one basket. To appoint a director to the board of a company in which the investor had a large shareholding would mean the appointment of a large number of people of the right type, and this would be very difficult to achieve. Furthermore, the investment managers are themselves managers and not entrepreneurs. In general it is the directors who are supposed to guide the managers in their own businesses, and they are hardly likely to be guided by managers from another business.

The second reason is that the institutional investors disclaim any technical knowledge of the industries in which they invest, and this is not surprising in view of the wide spread. They can hope only for a financial flair in making the right choice. (Some insurance companies do specialise; for example some become experts on property, but here it is generally direct investment in the actual property.) Like the small investor they must take the rough with the smooth, hoping for a good average return. Whereas the small investor can get out, if he recognises the signs of trouble in time, by selling on the stock exchange, the large investor is tied in. Any attempt at selling a large block of shares would depress the price against the seller.[4] It must be clear that selling the shares is not a remedy for the shareholders as a whole; the sale can be effected only by someone else becoming a shareholder.

Spey Investments was set up in 1967 as a private company to invest institutional funds mainly in private companies and new market ventures instead of the usual stock market purchase. Some of the main shareholders (in 1971) were the pension funds of ICI, Royal Insurance, Barclays Bank, the electricity supply industry, a group controlled by the J. Lyons families and Unilever. The Unilever pension fund pulled out in June 1971 and withdrew its cash, and in July the founder and shaper of Spey Investments sold his controlling interest to the institutional shareholders and severed all connection with the group, 'because of a genuine difference of opinion on policy' and after 'amicable discussions'. One reason for the genuine difference was evident in August, when the accounts were published. The investment group lost £79,000 on dealing (this was after payment of interest of £300,000 on money borrowed from the institutions, the main shareholders) and the trading group made a direct loss of £726,000, plus a write-off of £237,000. In eighteen months over £1 million was lost.

Now and again the institutions express their displeasure. When Rank made its bid for De la Rue in 1969 it was reported that a number of institutional investors in Rank disapproved of the bid as being against their interest. The reason was that they had bought Rank solely for the earnings growth expected from Rank Xerox and not because they had any faith in Rank's managerial ability in other fields (*Sunday Times*, 2 February 1969). This report also made the valid point that while shareholders in a bid-for company can accept or reject the bid, the shareholders in the bidding company seldom have any opportunity of stopping their company making the bid. Some very large losses have occurred to shareholders because managers have enlarged their empires by acquisitions that have turned sour.

When Dufay Bitumastic made a bid for International Paints in 1968 optimistic profit forecasts were issued. The realised profits were less than half of the estimate and the following year produced a loss. The result was that the institutional investors forced an investigation by a firm of accountants. (The institutions had stuck with Dufay even when its profit forecasts had been derided by Courtaulds at the time of the bid.) And in 1969 the institutions deposed the founder and the board of the building firm of Bradley of York after large losses (*Sunday Times*, 1 June 1969).

The *Daily Telegraph* made some telling criticism of pension funds, when in a controversial election for a director of British Printing the funds abstained from voting – 'not to know is pathetic' – and mentioned the alarmingly poor judgment in backing Spey with some £50 million. 'Is it a coincidence that the major shareholders left in Pergamon Press are pension funds? I have heard a remark attributed to one of the biggest pension fund managers: "What we've dropped on Pergamon is nothing to our losses in Rolls-Royce" ' (*Daily Telegraph*, 24 July 1971).

Conflicts of interest

Directors of public companies are in a position of trust and have a duty to the shareholders in the company which must override their own interests. There is the obvious duty of not making secret dealings in the company's shares based on internal information, or dropping hints to their friends to do so. On the whole the standard of honesty in such matters is considered high; in fact directors face more criticism for their competence than for their probity. The well-known cases of fraud are far more 'entrepreneurial' than 'directorial'.

Conflicts can occur where directors have other and connected business interests. The classic type of case is where the head of a company sells to that company his other business ventures which have gone wrong (William Lever was good at this) and if he is in a dominant position the other directors may not be too critical.

A similar position arises where a young or 'junior' director, who perhaps owes his position to the chief, is not satisfied with the way in which the company is being operated. To press the point too far may damage his career; not to press it may damage his sleep. Yet we have seen examples of where even the revered founders have been ousted by their fellow directors. Such is human nature – or a disinterested devotion to the affairs of the company – that the stab in the back often comes from a favourite who owes his position to the victim.

Another possible area of conflict is where the directors give themselves service contracts with the company. As directors they are subject to triennial re-election, but a long-service contract as a manager would mean that they could not be dismissed from the company without a considerable sum of money in compensation. This contrasts with the sometimes shabby treatment of minority shareholders in subsidiary companies, where the profits may be used for the benefit of the holding company.

A major area of conflict of interest occurs with takeover bids. The duty here is plainly to the shareholder, either to see that he is not despoiled, or if he is, that the price paid is as high as possible. But the better the fight put up the less will the director endear himself to the victor in a successful bid. In an 'agreed merger' the gates have been opened and suitable arrangements can be made. Where the fight is intensive and prolonged the director knows that the signal for no quarter is hoisted and that no prisoners will be taken. Victorious generals often show clemency and consideration to the generals they have defeated, but wars with paper money are often fiercer than those with real weapons. Some of the defences put up, at personal cost, notably by AEI, reflect great credit on those who have looked after the interests of the silent mass of shareholders and the career prospects of their own employees.

In spite of current disquiet about boardroom efficiency, it is difficult to make hard and fast rules about the composition and operation of the boards of companies. For every rule there is an exception. Stodgy old boards stuffed with titles make a profit, and young dynamic boards go straight down the slope. Attempts at improving the performance by legislation come up against the difficulty, as report after report on company law makes plain, that directors cannot be made efficient by Act of Parliament and attempts to tighten the law so as to catch the rarer cases of the fraudulent may make it difficult for honest men to accept office as directors.

Notes

1 Sir Joseph Latham, *Take-Over. The Facts and Myths of the GEC/AEI Battle,* p. 22.
2 Peter Wilsher, 'Call for a shareholders' ombudsman', *Sunday Times,* 23 May 1971.
3 Charles Babbage, *A Comparative View of the Various Institutions for the Assurance of Lives,* John Murray, 1826.
4 This point was made by the Prudential and other institutional investors in 1972 with regard to their investments in the Distillers Co. during the Thalidomide dispute. A large investor can sell in small parcels only as the opportunity arises. The opportunity is less if the company is in trouble.

Five

The scale of operations

> When trade is bad and he is making losses, when his fortune and his reputation alike are at hazard, his mind is fixed on avoidance of disaster; sleep deserts him on his bed.
>
> It is otherwise with the salaried manager. When he has done his day's work and goes home in the evening, he sleeps sound, conscious of duty done.
>
> But the sleepless nights of the entrepreneur are not unproductive.
>
> Von Thunen[1]

The modern, large-scale business unit is of comparatively recent origin. Admittedly, there have been previous cases of large firms. The East India Company started as an organisation of traders undertaking separate voyages and grew until it became a governing body ruling almost half of the sub-continent of India. The nineteenth-century railway companies were large businesses, both in capital and in numbers of people employed. Yet in 1921 there were still 214 separate railway companies in Britain though many were quite small and were operated by larger companies. The 1921 Railway Act combined 121 of them into larger groupings – the four main-line companies. It was not until after the Second World War that these four were combined into one large organisation, the British Transport Commission. In the interwar years the Central Electricity Board was created to control the generation and large-scale distribution of electricity through the grid system, although there were hundreds of firms, company and municipality, which sold the electricity to the public. They also owned the power stations, but their operation was controlled by the CEB which bought current from the producers. There were likewise hundreds of local authority and company suppliers of gas – large businesses which mainly followed the municipal boundaries.

There were other large firms in the nineteenth and early twentieth centuries. Some expanded by natural growth where the economies of scale justified the larger size. A main cause of growth was the amalgamation of different businesses into larger units, successful or otherwise. But generally the large firms, or what were then thought to be large firms, were exceptional peaks in a general landscape of small and moderate-sized family businesses, often under the master's eye.

The reason for this comparative smallness was that many of the important firms were still family businesses with a tradition of independence. To form a public company, to obtain limited liability in case of failure, and to shift part of the burden on to an unsuspecting public offended the scruples of some Victorians. A typical comment when a rival firm went public was, 'I did not know they were in such a bad way.' With certain exceptions the economy was very competitive, especially in the dominant trades such as cotton exports, iron and steel, ship-building and coal mining. The amalgamations that had taken place gave no grounds for believing in the superiority of the larger firm, and if it were less efficient there were plenty of competitors waiting. But the strong limiting factor was the policy of free trade. One powerful motive for increasing the size of the firm is to gain control of the market, and the smaller the market the better. Any such development in Britain could be countered by the free import of the monopolised goods. Free trade worked the other way also. Such a large proportion of British manufacture was exported that the world was the market and it could not be controlled. When Britain reversed her free trade policy in the 1930s the ground was prepared for the growth of monopoly and the larger business unit.

A feature of industry today, especially since 1945, has been the growth in size of the business unit, both of the joint-stock company and the public board. In many cases the latter have a virtual monopoly in the supply of their product (railways, gas, electricity and coal), a position which the companies may envy and seek to emulate.

There is here one very popular misconception, which many expanding businessmen do little to dispel. In some industries there are technical reasons why the plant should be operated at a certain minimum size, and further economies if a larger scale of operations is achieved. Examples are blast furnaces, oil refineries, chemical plants, other process plants, and ships. It does not necessarily follow, although it may do so in some circumstances, that there are further economies of operation if two or more plants are combined into the one business unit. The arguments for scale are in all the textbooks but they often fail to distinguish between the plant and the business unit.

If for example there are two chemical plants owned by two separate companies, each large enough to achieve full economies of operation so that each is operating at its technical optimum, there are no further technical economies to be achieved if the plants are combined into one business unit with the same plants operating as before. One argument is that the plants can work together, but they could do that under separate ownership. Prewar, when the CEB controlled electricity generation and the local municipalities or companies controlled distribution to the consumers, the industry worked as an economic unit with decentralisation of administration. It is not essential that there be a single railway system under a single management for people to travel from one part of the country to another. The prewar railway companies evolved clearing arrangements so that a traveller passed from one company to another, often without knowing that the company to whom he had paid his fare at the start of his journey was not the company which finally delivered him to his destination.

This is not the important issue today. Largely through amalgamations and takeovers the whole character of business is changing. Formerly the family business was a shop or a steel works or a cotton mill. It grew and became registered as a company but it was still a shop company, a steel company, or a cotton company. It was an identifiable business unit. Now the company can be anything and the title is no guide to the trade carried on. We have the multi-plant, multi-product company which makes a variety of goods in a large number of different factories. The only unifying factor is that it is all controlled by one impersonal corporate body.

The effects of the nineteenth-century Companies Acts, conferring corporate status and limited liability on any seven persons[2] who choose to register themselves as a business, have only recently made themselves fully felt.

In the large companies ownership and control have become separated. We are dealing here with general tendencies; early chapters have shown that the owner-entrepreneur-manager still survives. The shareholder-owners are numerous and widely scattered. The directors may represent sectional interests; they may have little financial stake in the profitability of the company, and the business is too large for them to manage it directly or adequately. Thus we have the directors determining policy and the managers carrying it out – the so-called Managerial Revolution or the Rise of the Professional Manager.

What exactly does this emphasis on professional management mean?

It cannot mean the distinction between the amateur and the professional such as exists in sport,[3] i.e. that the amateur is unpaid. The owner-manager was certainly paid, and paid by results. Directors are paid for their services, and there is even the 'professional' director who holds directorships in different companies.

The expression is used to mean, by implication, efficient management. The modern manager, who takes up the craft as a profession, is introducing a new concept of efficiency in business affairs. But this is to beg the whole question; is the operation of large companies, and public boards, more efficiently conducted by managers of other people's money than if the operation is in the hands of people with a financial stake in the results? It is interesting that when the managers look below themselves to the manual workers instead of upwards to the directors, they often believe in suitable financial incentives, and are only too ready to introduce various types of 'payments by results' schemes. The alleged efficiency of management will be examined later.

'Professional manager' also appears to mean that the manager is specifically educated and trained for his task. Again this is to beg the question, and to produce a predetermined answer to a question which has not been properly formulated. A particular way of producing managers which happens to be fashionable at the moment is not necessarily better than, say, the traditional way of learning on the job and promoting the most capable. It is not necessarily worse; all that is said here is that the issue is yet to be decided.

If we mean that in industry today the business unit is too big for the owner to undertake all the necessary supervision himself, this is quite true but it is not new. Large enterprises and activities have always employed others to carry out the administration of the policies. What is new is the extended use of the word 'manager' and 'management' and these trip off the tongue like the blessed word Mesopotamia. Stewards, bailiffs, officers, officials, governors, satraps and even clerks (the educated 'clerics' who could write) all performed some or all of the functions of management. Now apparently everyone is a manager, if only an assistant to a manager of a small sub-section. (The author once overheard a man being asked what he did at XY – a well-known company stuffed with managers, which has since gone bankrupt – and he replied that he had a unique job there, he was the only one in the organisation who was *not* in charge of something!)

With the growth in size there is a larger proportion of managers compared with owner-managers and peasant farmers, but this is only a change in degree and not in kind. It is also true that with a larger proportion of decisions being taken by managers their efficiency or otherwise becomes of greater importance.

The problem was first seen in estate management. This is more than a bit of farming. Large estates have comprised agriculture, mining, power supplies and industrial activities. When wealth was mainly in the form of land rather than paper claims to wealth, the rich were rich because of the number and extent of their estates. How were large estates to be managed?

Gibbon summarised the Roman solution like this:

> According to their temper and circumstances, the estates of the Romans were either cultivated by the labour of their slaves, or granted for a certain and stipulated rent to the industrious farmer. The economical writers of antiquity strenuously recommend the former method wherever it may be practicable; but if the object should be removed by its distance or magnitude from the immediate eye of the master, they prefer the active care of an old hereditary tenant, attached to the soil and interested in the produce, to the mercenary administration of a negligent, and perhaps an unfaithful, steward.

The problem can be approached in three ways: manage directly; hive off the management (decentralise); or employ professional managers. The first is the more common. What has survived of Xenophon's *Economics* (it must be remembered that the word meant the management of the household) is an analysis of how the administration of an estate, comprising agriculture and manufacture, is to be divided between the husband and the wife: a clear example of managerial specialisation. At a later date we have the great eighteenth-century landowners, who cultivated their own home farms and introduced new methods, and by their example spread the knowledge to their tenant farmers and brought about the Agricultural Revolution in Britain. In the nineteenth century there were the Prussian Junker farmers, 'the cultivating squires' who like the early Romans alternated between direct agricultural management and politics. It was from this class that Bismarck came. It is of course the method generally employed by the owner-manager in industry at all times.

Hiving off the management, decentralising the decisions, and relying on a financial link is to be found in the typical landlord and tenant relationship in British agriculture. Instead of the owner being responsible for the direct administration of all his estates he puts in tenant farmers in exchange for a money rent. In some cases, as in the French *métayage*, the rent can be proportional to the product. The English tradition has been for the landlord to provide the fixed capital in land and buildings, and for the tenant to provide the working capital in the form of stock.

But the best example of the solution to the problem, by obtaining the benefits of a large-scale, specialised industry with small-scale, decentralised 'shirt-sleeve' administration is to be found in the domestic, the merchant capitalist or the putting out system, as it is variously called. This is little known and less understood.

From the fourteenth to the eighteenth century England was the leading country in the greatest European industry, the manufacture of woollen cloth. Originally it had been a town industry with the entrepreneurial functions being performed by the master. But this guild-ridden, restrictive-practised industry declined in the face of the competition of a scattered country-wide industry making use of water power and being free of 'union rules'. The merchant bought wool from the farmer, took it by packhorse to the cottages where it was spun by the spinsters; he then took the wool to the weavers; from there to the water-operated fulling mill; from there the cloth was taken to market and eventually reached London or one of the export ports for the Continent. (There were slight variations in the Yorkshire industry but these do not concern us here.) The ramifications of the industry extended from small villages in Devon and the Cotswolds right across Europe without any overriding large-scale administrative organisation. It was a market economy. The merchant bought the wool, he paid the weavers (or independent weavers such as George Eliot's Silas Marner bought yarn and sold the finished cloth to the merchant), and he sold to the London merchant.

This principle is at work when a manufacturer decides whether to make an article himself within his own administrative organisation, or whether he is going to buy the article from another firm. The modern motor-car industry is an assembly industry, putting together the thousands of items made by large and small firms. The modern merchant-capitalist is exemplified by Marks and Spencer which orders goods to its own specification from independent manufacturers. In both cases it is largely a buying or commercial skill and not a manufacturing skill.

A company considering the problem of transporting its goods can either set up its own transport department, with a director of transport, transport manager, deputy transport manager, assistant to the transport manager, each with his bevy of secretaries, or it can buy its transport from the railways or independent carriers. The successful railway builders, such as Thomas Brassey, largely used the method of subcontracting part of the work. The many separate railway companies worked together by settling their accounts with each other through the railway clearing house.

It is interesting that when a large multi-activity company gets in an administrative tangle, which is not infrequent, it tries to create within itself the efficiency advantages of the market economy. It sets up separate independent administrative units. It establishes 'profit centres' where it tries to allocate the costs and profits of each particular operation. It discontinues operations such as when a manufacturing business with its own shops decides to sell them and deal with independent retailers, or when a particular manufacture or service is abandoned in favour of purchasing the goods or service. Sometimes goods are transferred from one process to another at the prices ruling in the market and the supplying department has to justify itself by this profit test. In rarer cases the using department is free to give the work to an outsider if that is cheaper.

It is the third method, that of direct management through the owner's stewards, bailiffs, clerks, officials, and now managers, which is tending to be the predominant form in modern industry with the growth in the size of the company, the public board and the activities of governments. Of course the entrepreneur in other forms employs managers, but the change in emphasis is significant and important.

Armies when small were under the direct command of the king, who generally charged with his men. When they became larger he had to go farther back so as to be able to supervise the conduct of the whole battle. With the specialisation into different units, infantry, slingers, archers, cavalry, siege trains, etc., it was necessary to have subordinate commanders for the different sections, which while acting separately were part of a strategic whole. It was here that the 'management' problems began to develop, seeing that each unit was in the right place at the right time, and could be relied upon to carry out instructions and not go off on private plunder.

The principle is to have a chain of command, so that each man knows to whom he is responsible and there can be units of different managerial sizes for different purposes. For example, according to Xenophon counting on the fingers of two hands, the divisions of Cyrus's army were:

	form	*under*	
5 men	1 squad	corporal	5
2 squads	1 sergeant's squad	sergeant	10
5 sergeant's squads	1 platoon	lieutenant	50
2 platoons	1 company	captain	100
10 companies	1 regiment	colonel	1,000
10 regiments	1 brigade	general	10,000

With modifications in the numbers in different units, this is the principle on which armies have been organised. The general does not have to control 10,000 men directly, he controls the ten regimental colonels, and so on. In modern armies this would be considered an excessive span of control and two or three armies would form an army group, but the principle remains. Split the task up into manageable proportions and do not have an excessive span of control so that real control is lost.

Following Cyrus, we can see how principles and solutions discovered in one form of human institution can be utilised in others. After his conquests (or successful takeover bids) he had the problem of administering a vast empire without incurring a mental breakdown.[4]

> And he thus pondered how the business of administration might be successfully conducted and how he might still have the desired leisure, he somehow happened to think of his military organisation: in general, the sergeants care for the ten men under them, the lieutenants for the sergeants, the colonels for the lieutenants, the generals for the colonels, and thus no one is uncared for, even though there be many brigades; and

when the commander-in-chief wishes to do anything with his army, it is sufficient for him to issue his commands only to his brigadier-generals. On the same model then, Cyrus centralised the administrative functions also. And so it was possible for him, by communicating with only a few officers, to have no part of his administration uncared for. In this way he now enjoyed more leisure than one who has care of a single household or a single ship.

When he had thus organised his own functions in the government, he instructed those about him to follow the same plan of organisation.

In this way, then, he secured leisure for himself and for his ministers.

The Victorian churchgoing businessman would be more familiar with the Old Testament story. Moses's father-in-law, Jethro, was appalled to see Moses sitting from morning to night hearing cases and settling disputes. The work was too much for one man and he advised the appointment of assistants, and:[5]

> Moses chose able men out of all Israel, and made them heads over the people, rulers of thousands, rulers of hundreds, rulers of fifties and rulers of tens. And they judged the people at all seasons: the hard causes they brought unto Moses, but every small matter they judged themselves.

This principle of delegation, to avoid excessive loading on the superior, is quite clear and simple. It is, however, difficult in practice. Many businessmen, especially the successful and energetic, such as William Lever, find it difficult to delegate. There are the businessmen who must see every piece of correspondence and sanction every item of expenditure; the college head who must approve every examination paper, including those of which he is completely ignorant. Others view their job, not as doing everything themselves but as having the right deputies and relying on them to do the work.

This is the second part of the problem. It is not sufficient to produce an organisation and to place people in various parts of that organisation. They have to be the right people. Xenophon commented on Cyrus's appointment of officers in charge of his various departments:[6] 'It is the same with these institutions as with everything else: whenever the officer in charge is better, the administration of the institutions is purer; but when he is worse, the administration is more corrupt'; and Jethro stressed the importance of the correct appointments by advising Moses to appoint 'able men such as fear God, men of truth hating covetousness'.

In fact 'it is men, not walls, that make the city' and the form of the organisation has always been a lesser problem than that of obtaining competent, and honest, officials or managers. 'If a man have two true servants, a man servant and a woman servant, he has a great treasure' is the judgment expressed by Fitzherbert.[7]

The use of the professional manager was widespread. It was evident in the feudal system established at the Conquest; William's followers were rewarded with land in proportion to their importance, but he had the opportunity, and the wisdom, not to give an individual too much land in one area. A baron rewarded with a number of manors would none the less be given ones in different parts of the country, which made it more difficult for him to create local pockets of independence. The lords had to live off the land; but as militarists few had either the inclination or the opportunity to be agricultural experts. They travelled from manor to manor, to enjoy the hunting and produce, but the administration was usually left in the hands of an agent.

A number of guides to husbandry and estate management have survived and these would be the medieval equivalent of managerial textbooks. We can see from these the various officials and their duties. The seneschal was the general manager of all the estates. The bailiff was in charge of each manor, and all the bailiffs would be responsible to the seneschal. The bailiff was the actual 'works manager'. The bailiff worked through the provost who was responsible for the detailed day-to-day work of running the estate. According to one adviser, he should be elected by the workers as the best husbandman on the manor – a combination of shop-steward and foreman. Finally there were the auditors, who 'heard the accounts' and were a check on the work of the other officials. In addition there were many specialists on each estate – ploughmen, shepherds, haywards, etc. The parallel between an estate of many manors is very close to that of a modern joint-stock company with branch factories or shops throughout the country, not subject to the direct control of the owners.

As the Middle Ages progressed, this system began to decay. The growth of a money economy in place of an economy based on direct services, and inflation in part due to the influx of silver from the New World, had their effects. The nobles became more and more separated from their estates, relying on the money rents received. The large estates tended to become a source of expenditure rather than a source of income. The number of dependants increased, magnificent houses were built, endless hospitality was offered to neighbours, there was attendance at court and the maintenance of a town house to pay for, so that the nobles got into debt to maintain themselves according to the requirements of their station in life. One can see the parallel in many large corporations, as Professor Parkinson has pointed out – the increase in head office staff, costly and magnificent head offices, the expense account hospitality and time spent on public affairs. Where the nobility were unable to pay their debts the estates were sold to a new kind of landowner who cultivated the land for profit – the failing company taken over.

The greatest example of professional management was to be found in the medieval church, particularly within the monasteries. In a celibate profession sons could not succeed their fathers – at least not openly. Nepotism was the nearest that could be achieved. One medieval bishop who married off his 'nieces' to the nobility was rumoured to have had closer family ties with the ladies. The student of management can detect a very close relationship between the administrative problems and history of the monasteries with that of the modern large joint-stock company.

Each order was founded by a man of enthusiasm who attracted similar followers. They took the vows of poverty, obedience and chastity, and combined a life of faith with hard work. Such, with some modifications, are the virtues of the self-made founders of firms. As the monasteries became older and richer the fire of the original enthusiasm burned dimmer. The monks abandoned manual work and paid servants appeared in every monastery. The work became divided into various departments, known as obedientiaries, and a monk of reasonable ability could hope to rise to be the equivalent of a modern departmental manager. The abbot became separated from the monks in the same way as the business owner who no longer works with his coat off alongside his employees, but occupies a separate office protected by his secretary.[8]

We find the modern equivalent of the 'golden handshake' where provision was made for the abbot who wished to retire. He had a set of rooms, domestic help, good food, and a settled income for private expenses. Accommodation was also let out. Under the corrody system a man could be relieved of the burden of administering his estates and settle with his wife and servants in the peaceful surroundings of a monastery. The cash payment was truly a godsend to an abbot who was desperate for a little ready money.

The established monastery had many sources of income yet many of them got into a chaotic financial state.[9]

> Over and over again we come across mismanagement and recklessness plunging a house into debt from which it tries to get free by shortsighted policies which promise a quick return but do nothing to remove the real cause of the disaster. . . . Retrenchment of expenses the last resort when all other methods had failed.

This is the same story which is repeated in the history of modern business.

One method of dealing with this problem of poor financial management was to introduce a regular audit of the accounts. Another was to centralise the finances by appointing treasurers for the whole house instead of the departmental managers having control over their own money. This has a familiar ring in the modern world. But perhaps the most remarkable of all was that some monasteries and nunneries put their financial affairs into the hands of outsiders to keep them in order. The consultancy profession can claim a most distinguished origin.

But measures are no substitute for men. There is in monastic history a close parallel with the clogs to clogs pattern in business. The older monasteries fell into bad ways because they ceased to attract the right men.[10]

> As the abbeys grew and prospered the demands which they made upon men became less, while the attractions which they offered grew greater. Inevitably the type of man deteriorated, and what was meant to be a religious community became more and more a residential country club.

It was always difficult to reform an established religious order. The dedicated enthusiasts perforce founded new institutions which competed for talent with the old, before they too succumbed to hardening of the arteries. Modern business history shows how difficult it is to revitalise an ailing company. For this reason the takeover of an unsuccessful company by an active one often proves disappointing. The 'proved successful management' makes little impact on the acquisition. This is why it is often comparatively easy for a determined newcomer to break into an established market. He is competing only with large, once prosperous firms.

Although the Industrial Revolution was the age of the inventor and of the self-made entrepreneur, the influence of the professional manager must not be overlooked. The cotton industry started with such owner-managers as Arkwright and the Strutts. Later many of the new owners of cotton mills were merchants who integrated backwards into manufacturing to satisfy the growing demand for the product. They had little interest in the manufacturing process which was a means to an end. They employed professional managers, left the management to them, and often suffered the consequences.

On the whole the managers were poorly paid, receiving little more than the hands they supervised. The job was accepted because it was a valuable experience and the ultimate objective was for the manager to go into business on his own account. When Drinkwater interviewed Robert Owen for the position of manager of his mill, he was amazed at the salary that Owen demanded, but the latter proved by his own accounts that he was worth it. (Owen had the natural expectation of a partnership and when this fell through he and a group of associates bought the famous New Lanark Mills from David Dale, where Owen became the managing partner.)

Many of the absentee owners were taken for a ride by their professional managers.[11]

> Gentlemen manufacturers would profit by an understanding of the scientific principles behind their machinery, and should understand the technical as well as the commercial. Several individuals who have embarked vast fortunes in factories are to a very great extent the victims at least, if not the dupes, of scheming managers. . . . There are no doubt many mill managers perfectly fitted by judgment, knowledge, and integrity to second the sound commercial views of the mill owner, and to advance the business with a profitable career. These practical men form the soul of our factory system. But with a wrong headed, plausible manager, the proprietor is sure to be led such a mechanical dance as will bewilder him completely.

One of the most fascinating attempts to grapple with this problem of administration at a distance through professional managers was the famous Crowley Ironworks. An ironmonger in London, Crowley set up a nation-wide organisation. The head office and principal warehouse was in London and hundreds of workers were employed in factories near the Tyne. Goods were shipped to London, and from there they were sent to agents in the main naval dockyards or to warehouses in different parts of the country. Bar iron was bought in England, Sweden, Russia and America and finished products sold to the Navy, and to customers in England and in the American and West Indian colonies. The business was managed from the head office mainly by post.

This highly integrated business was under the single control of an autocratic if paternalistic entrepreneur. Every aspect of the organisation was regulated in detail, after the famous *Law Book*. (A modern equivalent would be a rule book, an instruction manual or a job specification.) The laws were mainly composed before 1700, and were revised at various dates. One section appeared as late as 1807.[12]

There is some dispute as to whether all the laws were enforced, or were even enforceable. The fact that they were constantly revised can be taken as evidence that they did not always work satisfactorily, but that they were in normal operation. A modern authority states that it is difficult to judge whether the business was successful because of the laws or in spite of them. There was such a mass of detail that 'working to rule' could have been as ineffective and inefficient as it is today.

In the administrative structure Crowley provided a system of management by committee, probably taking the view that the different members of each committee would act as a check on each other. There were committees (using modern terminology) for manufacturing, transport and subsidiary mills, a works council, and a social welfare committee (the Governors of the Poor), but Crowley was the ultimate court of appeal.

Crowley was a paragon of efficiency; Crowley's word was his bond, Crowley's goods were good, and Crowley delivered the goods. But his intolerance of the human frailties of others did not make him popular with his employees. His revisions of the laws were always accompanied by moral exhortations or criticisms. This was directed towards his managers and not to the general body of workmen, for he always insisted on the best possible labour relations.

His distrust of his officials can be seen in these extracts from the *Laws*:

'It hath by experience been found that where government or people leave the management of their business to any single person, that their interest suffereth from want of advice, their estate wasted for want of checks upon their managers' (New Law 83), and this prompted him to follow Solomon in deciding that 'in the multitude of counsellors is safety'.

He said of the sending of weekly reports to London, 'There is nothing more rude in any person than not to answer letters sent to them.'

'The office of a Cashier being a post that lys open to sundry temptations' . . . and 'I then found that sundry people I trusted with cash, for want of proving the same, gave opportunities to villans to make use of my money.'

Concerning stock control: 'Whereas I have found great miscarriage in some ironkeepers in the stocks of iron I have entrusted with them . . .' is followed by full instructions regarding the keeping and accounting of stocks.

'Whereas I have received great damage by reason of unskilfull, negligent, and corrupt Surveyors who (without regard to the great trust reposed in them) have not taken that due care to prevent errors in making of goods as they ought but have carelessly passed them by when made, without considering that goods ought to be made saleable, serviceable, and in every respect fit for their intended use' was an insistence on quality control. It is obvious that these strictures are reserved for the surveyors (inspectors?) and not for the workmen who may err through lack of proper supervision. Completed work was handed in and the workman credited with the value, less any abatements for bad work. It was the duty of the surveyors to do all they could for the workmen to prevent them running into errors. They were certainly not to be kept waiting as 'their time is their bread'. (See chapter 2 above for the business in later years passing into outside hands through marriage and being conducted by a family of managers until 1863.)

There were other 'professional managers'. At Coalbrookdale the sons, and sons-in-law, went into the business at the top, but the sons of chief clerks and foremen also joined the firm and eventually succeeded to their fathers' posts. In iron and steel in the nineteenth century there was the same pattern of near hereditary management. Where business ownership and direction became aristocratic with the owners being separated by wealth and outlook from the bulk of their employees there would be more reliance on the faithful steward. This could vary from the firm where the family directors took an active part, working through managers in subordinate positions, right up to the organisation where the family, often female inheritors, took no active part but employed a general manager to look after their patrimony.

Today then there is no difference in kind but only in degree. The larger firms have a larger corpus of managers in different ranks. Many of the directors are non-owners and are promoted managers. It is sometimes difficult to draw an exact line between the 'pure' director and the 'pure' manager. Many of the largest firms have at their head chairmen and managing directors who are in their positions not because of share ownership but because they have been promoted on their ability, or have come straight into the boardroom from other firms, the services or public administration. Many of them, and the reader can produce his own list, exhibit the entrepreneurial attitudes rather than the managerial. They are not managers in the narrow sense of carrying out other people's policies, but are businessmen with a commercial attitude. Some of the appointments to the postwar public boards have produced men of this type, who would be interchangeable with chairmen or managing directors of large public companies. But such people are comparatively rare, both in outstanding ability and in their commercial attitudes.

Notes

1 Quoted by Sir John Hicks in *A Theory of Economic History*. Clarendon Press, 1969, p. 117.
2 Sometimes they were described as 'any seven poverty-stricken rogues who chose to register a company'.
3 Football commentators appear to use the word to mean successful: 'Hackers United are *so* professional' – but they are playing against other professionals, who presumably are also *so* professional.
4 Xenophon, *Cyropaedia*, vol. 2, Loeb Classical Library, Heinemann, 1914, p. 313. These texts have the Greek on one page and an English translation facing, which is of benefit to those readers who are as ignorant as the present author of the original Greek.
5 *Exodus* 18: 25–6.
6 Xenophon, op. cit., p. 309.
7 Fitzherbert, *Book of Husbandry*, 1534.
8 'If abbots recovered their spirits when they were away from their monks, no doubt the monks also felt happier when they saw their father-in-God riding down the road and knew he would not be back for some months. . . . The abbot had become an august person

whose occasional visits to the monastery were associated in the minds of the monks with inspection, anxiety and discipline.' J. R. H. Moorman, *Church Life in England in the Thirteenth Century*, p. 275. Is there not the same anxiety when the managing director of a multi-plant firm makes his periodical visitation to the branch factory, with his bevy of assistants trailing the regulation two paces behind?

9 Ibid., p. 306.

10 Ibid., p. 254.

11 Andrew Ure, *The Philosophy of Manufactures*, H. Bohn, 1835, pp. 42–3.

12 M. W. Flinn, *The Law Book of the Crowley Ironworks*. My quotations are taken from the Surtees 1957 edition.

Six

The methods of business organisation

Business reorganisation – the substitution of measures for men.

Charles Wilson, *The History of Unilever*, p. 273

The student will be told that there are certain principles of management which are a guide to business success. He will be even more hopeful of reaching the promised land if he encounters 'scientific management', which of course appears to put these principles on a high intellectual plane. These principles, like the principles evolved in pure science, are as true and as unchanging as the laws of the Medes and Persians.

However, on further investigation he finds that there are no principles of organisation in the absolute sense that these are eternal verities of universal application. The economist covers the point in his own trade by declaring that economic laws are statements of tendencies which describe what is likely to happen in the generality of cases. Although circumstances admit exceptions, the laws are statistically true. We saw above that the 'law' of clogs to clogs in three generations, which has a proverbial and respectable ancestry and has strong reasons to support it, is one which is subject to many exceptions. Even in the pure sciences, such as physics, the laws of science are often no more than hypotheses, or first approximations, subject to revision or rejection on further study.

In the management of human affairs the search for absolute truth is even less rewarding. The principles of management, or the principles of organisation, are evolved as a result of experience, and often are common sense or proverbial statements guiding human conduct. But they are not absolute.

No principle, however well tried and proved by experience, will succeed in all cases. Pushing a principle to its extreme limit is dangerous, as Aristotle taught us in the science of ethics, virtue lies in a mean. The matter may be put in another way. We cannot assemble a series of formulae, or a number of equations of mathematical impeccability, and produce the ideal form of organisation to suit ICI or British Rail. These organisations can be, and have been, organised in many different ways – some people would say far too many ways. What can be said is that each method of organisation that may be tried has different characteristics but that there is no one answer which is right and the others are wrong. The solution to the problem, as economists would say, is indeterminate.

Bearing these warnings in mind, we can examine some of the organisation problems of modern business, and apply some of the 'principles'.

Span of control

The first principle is the span of control, which places a limit on human activity. No man can effectively control more than x other people. The value of x depends partly on the efficiency of the controller – some people cannot manage one other person and some people are managerial geniuses – and partly on the nature of the work. The span of control can be large where it is a question of supervising routine work and little interference is necessary; the galley master has to walk up and down the centre and see that all the galley slaves are pulling hard and in unison – any worker who rows faster than the others succeeds only in rocking the boat. The span of control will be much smaller where the work of the subordinates interacts, where what A does affects the work of B and C. There are individuals with conflicting ends and pressures, whose activities have to be co-ordinated.

A common and important example of this problem is the necessity for co-ordinating production with sales. What is produced must be sold and what is sold must be produced by the organisation. Someone in authority must see that these two departments are controlled *vis-à-vis* one another. When this principle of co-ordination is broken we have the firm (in the jargon a production-orientated company) which produces those goods that are easier or more interesting and then hopes to sell them. It blames the customers, their philistine taste, or the government, if the company produces goods which the market does not want. Yet the manufacturing process is not complete until the product is finally sold. At the other end is the market-orientated company whose salesmen and directors accept orders that are difficult, impossible, or unprofitable to fulfil.

A large organisation must be broken down into units or cells of activity, and like the parts of a watch these units have to work together for the benefit of the whole. The component parts will vary in size. In a very large organisation, such as we are considering here in the main, there will be many such parts, far too many for each to be responsible to the one head, or for that head to control them all individually. The parts must be arranged in groups. The problem is how this grouping is to take place for the maximum effectiveness. In a simple example one man B is in charge of ten others, each A. The organisation chart will be:

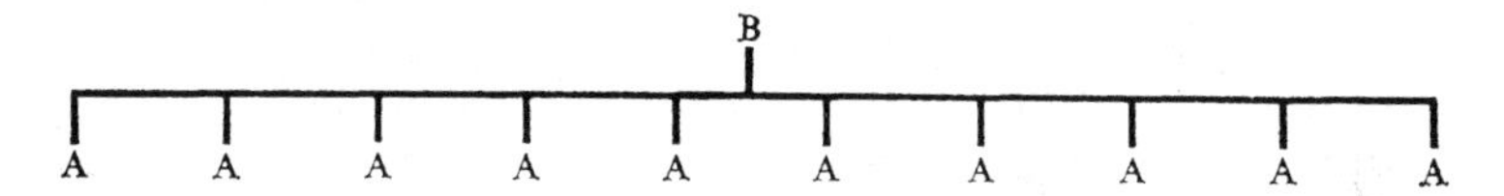

The work load expands and additional people are engaged so that B is now responsible for the work of eleven, then twelve, then thirteen people, etc. There comes the time when the span of control is excessive and no adequate supervision can be exercised, so an additional controller is introduced.

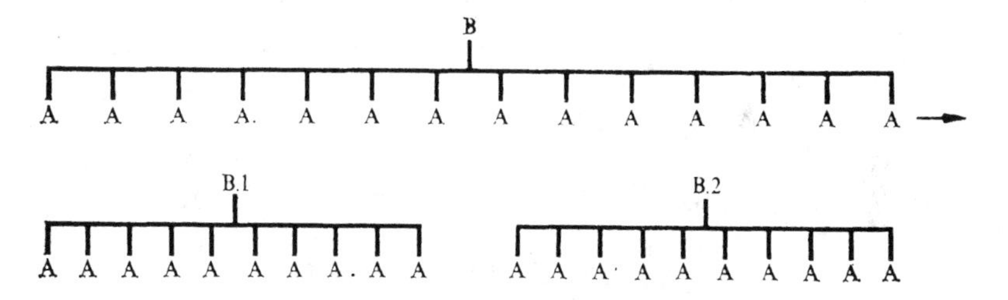

B.1 and B.2 are of equal rank and there must be co-ordination between them. This can be achieved by introducing a third rank, C, to whom B.1 and B.2 are responsible, thus:

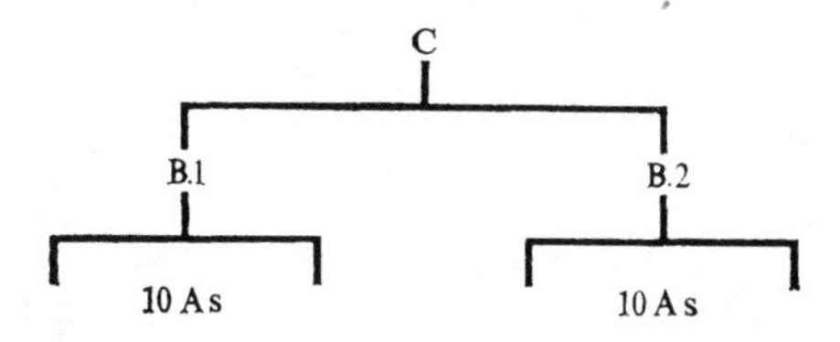

C is now probably underemployed and any further expansion in the firm can take place by adding more of the lower supervision, B.3, B.4, B.5, and so on. Depending on the difficulty of co-ordinating the work at the lower level, C's responsibilities can increase until his span of control becomes excessive. If he can control ten Bs, then this simple organisation would control 1,000 workers with two levels of management.

For 2,000 workers we would require two Cs and therefore an additional rank, D, to co-ordinate the Cs, but here again D would be underemployed at first, until the firm had expanded sufficiently to provide him with more Cs to chivvy. This is one reason why in any expanding organisation there is the need for periodical reorganisation, and why the expansion proceeds in fits and starts.

So we have the principle (which is elementary arithmetic) that the greater the span of control the fewer the management 'steps' in the organisation, and the smaller the number of managers necessary; and the smaller the span of control, the greater is the number of steps required for adequate management. We have seen this in the army of Cyrus where the span of control was either five or ten according to the level of management required. Generally speaking, lower down in the organisation, the work is simpler, and the span of control greater; higher up in the organisation the work is more complicated and responsible, and the span of control is smaller.

If we reduce the number of steps there is the danger of excessive span of control, resulting in the overloading of executives and inadequate control. If we reduce the span of control, there are more links in the management chain, more levels through which information has to pass, a slowing down in operations and excessive bureaucracy. There are no principles as such which will give us the right number of people at each level; there is only a balance of advantages and disadvantages with each variation in this type of organisation.

Line management

This type of organisation is known as the hierarchical, the military or the line, because it is typical of the organisation of a church, especially the Catholic Church, and of armies. Very large organisations can be built up in this way by increasing the steps in the chain of command, which is not to say that such an organisation would be effective and efficient in all circumstances.

The merit of this form of organisation, when properly applied, is that a clear line of authority and instructions can be passed down from the top to the bottom and no one is omitted; and the responsibilities of each member of the organisation are clearly defined. D gives orders to C; each C gives orders to each B under him. There is no conflict of duty or supervision. Each B is responsible for the work of the ten As under him, and each A receives instructions from his own immediate superior only. While all Bs are superior in rank to all As, only one B has actual authority over one particular group of As; he is their immediate commanding officer. A bishop has jurisdiction over the priests in his diocese; no other bishop can interfere inside that diocese. The principle is quite clearly understood in army organisation but not so clearly understood or applied in commercial practice.

Those in subordinate positions are responsible to one immediate superior so that there can be no confusion as to their duties. It is also a rule that if C wishes a particular A to carry out a task, he does not instruct directly but tells the appropriate B, who passes the instruction to A. In any case B is responsible for the work that A does.

The rule is alas broken in industry with harmful effects. The works manager gives direct instructions to a workman, interfering with the work he was already in the process of doing. The foreman slates the workman for not doing the job that he, the foreman, thought he was doing. The workman gleefully replies that he received his instructions from the works manager. The foreman's authority over his staff is damaged. The managing director who says his door is always open may give an impression of democratic *bonhomie* but he is in danger of not having an effective middle management. Where responsibility is exercised the necessary authority must be delegated, and not arbitrarily interfered with. The man on the spot must be supported or removed.

Likewise the conferment of the proper authority carries with it the full responsibility for the operation. Each manager or official is responsible for the work carried out by his subordinates under his instructions. This principle is clearly seen in the doctrine of ministerial responsibility where the minister in Parliament has to answer for all the actions of his department. Sometimes this may appear harsh, as in the Crichel Down case where the Minister of Agriculture was let down by the advice he received from the civil service (and the agents it employed) and, to use the expressive term, 'he carried the can' and had to resign. But how often do we see the head of a department taking credit for all that goes well and blaming his subordinates when something goes wrong! Sometimes the head will reserve to himself the pleasant tasks and delegate to his assistant the more unpopular ones.

There is the contrary view too:[1]

> The duty of pronouncing censure, using coercion, inflicting pains and penalties on those who come short in any respect, is one that must of necessity give rise to a certain amount of unpopularity. Therefore my sentence is that a great ruler should delegate to others the task of punishing those who require to be coerced, and should reserve to himself the privilege of awarding the prizes. The excellence of this arrangement is established by daily experience.

The limitations of the line organisation are lack of information, bureaucracy and lack of specialised skill.

First I shall take failure to get correct information and act upon it. The basis of the system is that orders pass down the line and information passes up. It is the lower ranks who are closest to the enemy and the generals who are farthest away from the scene of the action. The information passes back through many channels and is subject to delay and constant interpretation, or misinterpretation, at each stage. The information may be ignored because it comes from an inferior in the organisation. The general who is convinced that he is opposed by a small squadron of light armoured cars, and has made his plans accordingly, does not like to be told by a scout with the rank of corporal that round the hill is the finest concentration of heavy tanks in the history of warfare. The manager who gets reports from his salesmen that the reason orders are falling off is that the competitors have introduced a superior product, may refuse to believe them. He treats them to a long discourse on how when he was on the road he could sell anything. The reason for the decline in sales may not be as the salesmen say. The point is that no one has yet found out the true facts. There is other information which would be welcome at headquarters but it is not worth the salesmen's while to pass it on; they are paid a commission on sales and not on market research.

Second, there is red tape. The larger the organisation and the longer the scalar chain the more rigorous the application of rules to ensure that each executive acts in the manner required by the organisation. There must be common policies so that all similar cases can be treated alike. Therefore there must be rules to be obeyed. In a given situation the written instructions have to be followed or a superior consulted. In the civil service the reason is quite obvious. The service carries out the law as laid down by Parliament and the same law must apply to all. If an old lady in Brighton is allowed a concessionary pension to which she is not entitled under the Pension Acts, all old ladies in Bootle and Bolton who are in the same circumstances will be justifiably aggrieved if they do not receive the same concession.

The area sales manager who gives a special discount to a customer who by chance happens to be a member of the same golf club is, at best, making a mockery of his company's marketing and pricing policy, elaborated after much travail by the head office. Nothing is more likely to cause dissatisfaction and industrial unrest than the suspicion that some favoured workmen are getting extra money.

Where it is true that doing the right thing is no more than is expected of the official, and doing the wrong thing is a cause of anxiety, trouble and memos from above, it is no wonder that an element of caution creeps in. It is better to be slow and reach the right decision than to be enterprising and be proved to be wrong. This is not to be taken as a criticism of the system. In the circumstances outlined keeping to the rules means observing the rule of law and the citizen gets what he is entitled to get. He is not dependent on the good nature or the rapacity of the official. The system is appropriate in large organisations where the pattern of activity changes little. It is less useful where circumstances are changing quickly. Well-managed armies and navies get round this problem by training their officers to exercise initiative where necessary. 'Turning the blind eye' to instructions is a tradition since Nelson – shooting the unsuccessful 'pour encourager les autres' is less frequent.

The third defect in this type of organisation is that it does not develop and make full use of specialised skills. All people at the same level are doing the same job with more or less the same efficiency. Specialists do not easily fit into the pure line organisation, so it has to be modified in practice.

Line and staff

The line organisation ensures that an agreed policy is carried out according to the rules. It does nothing to assess the correctness of that policy or to plan for changes necessary in policy or organisation when the circumstances alter. This is achieved by appointing people who are not responsible for executive action but who are responsible for thinking, planning and advising the senior executive.

An army on the march requires quarters for the night. Someone must go ahead when it is safe to do so and arrange food and lodging, the château for the general, the inn for the officers and the church or stables for the men. Arrangements for the supply of food en route have to be made, as do plans for ammunition and replenishments of footwear to be available. A campaign which entails crossing rivers would fail if the supply of pontoons had not been properly planned in advance. In the event of failure, provision for evacuation by the navy will be necessary. The quartermaster-general is one of the oldest of the specialist staff functions. It can be seen in Xerxes' invasion of Greece where there were huge problems of logistics with the large armies and fleets. (One adviser correctly forecast that the expedition would be defeated by the land and the sea rather than by the enemy but this defeatist and unpatriotic advice was ignored.) Marlborough and Napoleon both relied heavily on their chiefs of staff. It was 'Generals January and February' who defeated Napoleon in 1812, when the army was caught out in the winter without adequate food or shelter.

Industrialists have been slow to learn this lesson from military experience, but there has been a growth in the use of such departments as product research, market research (providing information upon which to act), production planning and control, marketing strategy (providing the detailed plans), and inspection, auditing and accounting (checking the results against the plans). To be effective there must be a complete separation between the functions of the line (executive) and the staff (advisory). The latter has no executive authority over the conduct of the operations. The staff advises the commander or managing director, and plans are put into operation because he approves of them and grants the necessary executive powers. (Note the word 'staff' here is used in the military sense of the staff officer and not in the general sense of the word to cover people who work in the office, are paid monthly, or who arrive at work at nine o'clock.)

Separating the planning and doing involves a new problem, that of co-ordinating their two functions. The army meets this problem by interchanging personnel. Officers considered suitable are sent to staff college to learn their craft, and then come back into a line appointment. Promotion may not be a steady move up the line, but a series of sideways and upward movements to gain experience of staff work and command. In commercial and industrial work the two functions tend to be more separated. Co-ordination is sought by meetings and joint committees between line and staff management.

Functional management

Another form of management organisation (or to be more precise, a different emphasis in management organisation) is the functional system. Here the emphasis is not on command or authority but on the possession of some specialised skill or technique, or on the carrying out of a particular task. This occurred in armies at an early date with the separation of function and difference in skills between the infantry and the cavalry, the slingers, archers and artillery. In navies there was the distinction between the sailors who operated the ships (or pulled at the oars) and the soldiers, or marines, who did the fighting. A modern warship carries a much larger number of specialists.

In a manufacturing plant there is the threefold division between production, marketing and the general administration of the company, corresponding to the work of the factory manager, the sales manager and the secretary. As firms grow larger a greater degree of specialisation leading to task efficiency becomes possible. Marketing is split into home sales and export sales; advertising, market research, packaging, public relations, product co-ordinators and others all produce new departments. The American engineer F. W. Taylor found that the foremen were performing eight separate functions, and these were being duplicated right across the line. A foreman might be good at one or two functions and fail in others, i.e. he might be a good disciplinarian but a poor organiser of work. Taylor did away with the traditional form of organisation and made each foreman responsible for a particular function and with no control over or responsibility for the others. They were given the functions of route clerk (routeing the work through the factory), instruction card clerk, cost and time clerk, gang boss, speed boss, inspector, repair boss and shop disciplinarian. One can compare the two systems, where in a small jobbing factory the foreman is given the blueprint or a general indication of what is required, decides how the job is to be done and instructs his own workmen, with that in a large mass-production factory, where the design department decides what is to be produced, the drawing office produces the detailed plans, another office routes the goods and materials through the factory, and yet another inspects the products.

While specialisation or division of labour produces greater efficiency, it does create new problems. These problems are difficult to solve in the sense of achieving a smooth-running organisation that is not in danger of breaking down; and difficult in the sense that 'solutions' are liable to be costly in facilities and in manpower. There is a growth in administrative staff *vis-à-vis* the 'line' or production.

The problem is essentially one of co-ordination. Instead of becoming easier the task becomes progressively more difficult with an increase in the size of the organisation. If there are only two people concerned, what X does affects Y only and there is one line of communication and one agreement or disagreement. If three people are concerned there are three lines, what X does affects Y and Z and what Y does affects Z. If there are four interdependents, the permutations increase to six; with five people there are nine, and with six there are fifteen permutations. The mathematically inclined can work out how many possibilities of disagreement exist when twelve people, each one with his own axe to grind, sit round a table to discuss a controversial policy. A product modification can affect design, purchasing, planning, routeing, advertising, sales instructions, catalogues, pricing, wage rates and bonuses, recruitment or redundancy, and stock-keeping.

A constant problem with functional organisation is the limitations of the functions and the drawing of boundaries. Something flows through the organisation, a product or a managerial idea. Different people or departments do something to it on its way. A task is split up into two separate jobs. Where should the line between them be drawn? Naturally each specialist department wants to retain as much power as possible. One sees this in the specialist functional management textbooks, where the importance of the function in the organisation is made clear, and sound reasons advanced why that particular function should have control over related or ancillary activities. Does the personnel department recruit people and allocate them to the different departments, or does the head of a department make his own appointments, or is there a compromise solution where the two departments co-operate to appoint a member that neither of them really wants? Does the works manager accept the designs from the office or does he tell it what he requires? The stores are located in the works to provide materials for production and at the same time to initiate records which are used for costing purposes. Do the clerks in the stores come under the factory manager or the accountant? Where does purchasing fit into the organisation? Does the works manager order his own supplies direct and the office manager buy his own office supplies or is there a specialised purchasing department to which both must make requests?

Specialist departments like to take over or retain all activities which are interesting, which offer scope for expansion, or which are traditionally theirs. Awkward or unpopular jobs tend to fall between two departments. A job may be done twice by two different departments or fail to be done at all. Departments which complain about the demands made on them for information will cheerfully maintain their own duplicate set of records.

This source of conflict is aggravated where the departments depend on different types of skills or professional knowledge or training. The first great divide is between the operations, the doers, and something known as the 'office'. The latter is often the means whereby the pronouncements from on high are translated into executive action. The resentment at the curtailment of function is directed against the office, or Kremlin as it is often termed. In some firms where the product is highly technological, there is bad blood between engineers and accountants, or between engineers or chemists and salesmen. Once this feeling exists it is almost impossible to eradicate, and newcomers are taught to form a circle and close ranks, like a herd of cattle with the horns outwards on the approach of wolves. Like Boston, where the Cabots speak only to Lowells and the Lowells speak only to God, loyalties to the department come first and to the company a long way second. Bitter rivalries between nineteenth-century railway companies persisted even after they were amalgamated by the 1921 Act. There is more joy when a rival department falls flat on its face than there is sorrow over the reduction of the dividend as a result of the misfortune.

A further source of inefficiency is the tendency of the specialist departments to increase in size and in number. If a man's importance in an organisation is largely judged on the number of people he controls, he will want to make that department bigger. If the communication system in the company necessitates attendance at a large number of committee meetings he will require an assistant to mind the shop while he is absent, or to send to the meeting if it promises to be particularly boring. If somebody at the top has a new idea – new to him – a department can be set up to put this idea into effect. If the originator dies, or retires, or loses interest the department may still continue, like the human appendix, a vestigial organ serving no useful purpose. The increase in the number of departments adds to the burden of the existing departments and they have to enlarge their own staff to cope with the problem.

When a firm is expanding it is easy for departmental heads to obtain sanction for an increase in their department due to pressure of work and this spreads through the organisation like bindweed. Sir Miles Thomas showed the reverse process in his autobiography. When he became managing director of BOAC it was necessary to retrench on expenses and staff. He found that this was putting Parkinson's law into reverse. A superfluous mid-level executive occupies an office that has to be heated, lit and cleaned. He has to have a secretary. He probably has an opposite number in another department with whom he corresponds, who also has an office, a secretary and expenses. Cutting down on one person probably saved the expense of another two or three people. 'When pruning in BOAC really got rolling we began to shed our fat at an almost visible rate.'[2]

When a firm runs into financial difficulties it can slaughter its executive suite like a usurper eliminating all the former king's relatives without any apparent loss of effectiveness. One can only assume that pruning strengthens the roots. But the work of the organisation still continues.[3] If a certain department is allowed when profits are high and is scrapped when profits fall, it makes no contribution to efficiency.

The general organisation chart (Fig. 1) shows in a very simplified form a model of an organisation. The owners, the shareholders, the state, or the members of a church, delegate authority to operate the organisation to a smaller body, the board of directors, the war office, or the church council. At the next level are the functional departments, production, sales, infantry, artillery, etc. Each of these will be organised through sub-managers, departmental heads, battalion commanders, ships' captains. Depending on size the lines can be extended downwards on the line principle.

Parallel to this organisation will be the staff functions, advising, planning, researching, auditing, and so on. They will operate at different levels, the chief of staff advising the commander-in-chief, but the ramifications of their work will extend downwards so that their juniors will be affecting the work of the functional departments and their sub-departments.

Thus there is no one pattern of organisation; all organisations are a mixture in various blends of the line, line and staff, and the functional. Some emphasise one aspect more than another; the armed forces emphasise the line of command, the highly

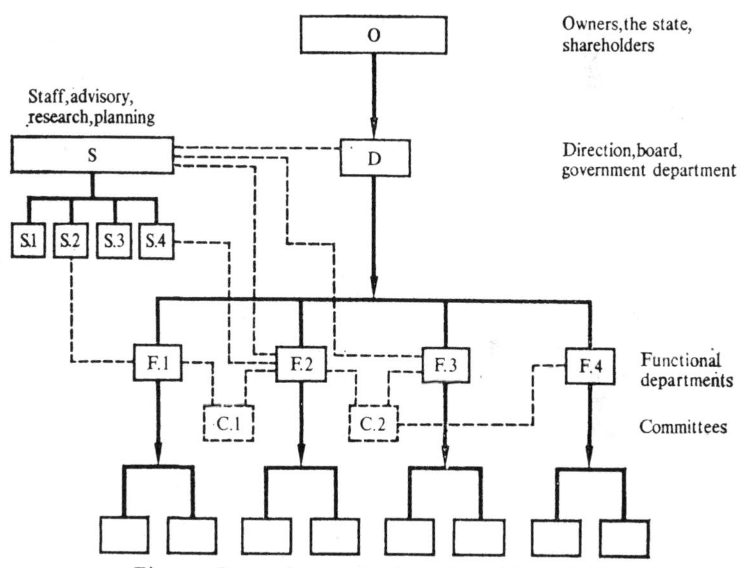

Fig. 1 General organisation chart (simplified)

technological industry will emphasise the specialist functions being performed. The unbroken lines on the chart indicate lines of authority, the dotted lines the staff relationships, and the broken lines communications on co-ordination. The relationship between D and F.1, F.2 . . . is a line-relationship, and so is the relationship between F.1 and its sub-departments below. Notice also that although the staff are advisory and not executive, a line organisation will exist within each staff department; there will be managers, assistant managers and others with a similar internal organisation to that of any executive department.[4] Where the work of F.1 affects the work of F.2 and F.3, and perhaps one or more of the staff departments, there must be some administrative machinery to achieve co-ordination. There may be interdepartmental conferences, policy meetings, committees, or just informal consultation between the interested parties.

The chart shows a few lines only to illustrate the principle, but every point on the organisation could be connected up to every other point. It represents a small organisation. With a larger organisation, shown on a larger chart, the interrelations become more numerous, and a whole network of lines showing interrelationships between different members of the organisation becomes extremely complicated.

This kind of organisation covers a single unit, a department store or a large factory. Many businesses today have a large administration because not all their work is concentrated in one

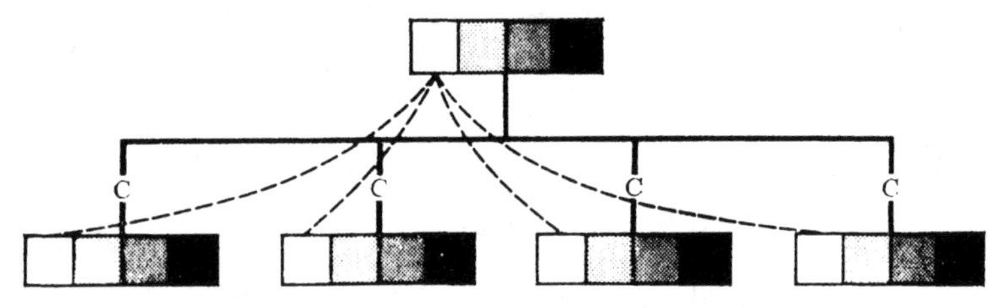

Fig. 2 Ship and fleet organisation

factory or production unit. Many different units or factories may be under the umbrella of the same company management. The main organisation chart would have to be multiplied horizontally with all the lines and functions and staff repeated. The problem now is the interrelation between the different units. A method of dealing with this follows the analogy of the ship and the fleet.

Each ship is a self-contained organisation with all the specialist functions on board. Two or more ships together are not just an increase in the number of operating units, they form a new entity, the fleet.

Each operating unit has a head, C – captain, branch manager, area manager, divisional manager. Under him are (for example) four separate functional heads: engineer officer, works manager, sales manager, personnel manager. (In practice there will usually be more than four separate specialities but four keeps the chart uncomplicated.) Each C is responsible to a head, admiral, general manager, divisional manager. The latter will have on his staff senior people in these various functions – fleet engineer, fleet medical officer, head office production department, general sales director, company personnel director, and so on.

What are the solutions to the problem of co-ordination of the specialist activities at the ship and the fleet level? The navy (like the army on administrative problems) is quite clear on this. The line of command goes down directly from the admiralty, through the base or command (the commands of the Nore or Spithead) to the fleet or smaller unit, and the captain of each ship is in sole command. He may consult his specialists but he does not have to accept their advice, right or wrong, he is held responsible for all decisions taken. He is the senior man on the spot and has full authority. There is one major point on which the comparison between a fleet and an industrial organisation breaks down. When it is necessary to have an admiral in charge of a number of captains, he cannot run alongside in an admiral's barge, directing operations. He has to be physically accommodated on one of the ships, preferably the most comfortable or powerful, but he is not in command of that ship any more than of any other ship in the fleet. That is still the responsibility of the captain. He does not directly interfere with the internal running of the ship even if his presence is distinctly effective on the flagship.

The heads of the functional departments are responsible to the captain for their actual operations, although they have a functional relationship with their seniors at the base or the fleet. And they move around. Servicemen in the navy do not serve in one 'factory' all their working lives. Ships are commissioned for a number of years and at the end of that period the various specialists will be posted to other commissions, and they may never see their former shipmates again. Thus their loyalties, rivalries and chances of advancement lie within their own branch of the service.

We have already touched on the possibilities of conflict between people exercising different specialist functions at plant level. These are increased when there is not the insistence on the line of command as takes places in the services, but where communication between the different management levels is direct. In the diagram of the fleet organisation, the dotted lines of the functional specialists come down through the command lines; but as shown above they go direct from the functional or staff departments at one level to the level below. It is similar to the functional foreman organisation of F. W. Taylor. Instead of being dotted lines they may become straight lines of command on a functional basis. The accountant, or personnel manager at area or plant level, has allegiance not to the local head but to a similar functional department at head office. This can mean a lack of co-operation at the operating level, especially where there are specialist professional talents being exercised, and where professional rivalries are rampant (see below for the Coal Board).

Centralisation and decentralisation

But the great unsolved problem is the degree of control to be exercised by the top management over the activities of those lower down in the organisation. An undertaking is centralised where the decisions are taken at the centre and lower management carries out orders. Cases outside the normal run have to be referred to the top for a decision. This is quite common in the expanding entrepreneur firm. The owner *knows* all the problems of all the departments. At one time he handled them all himself. He is in a position to decide on the merits of the problem. As he is an exceptional man, he distrusts the lesser abilities of his subordinates. There are exceptions, men who have built up businesses by finding the right man, giving him the authority, and leaving the management to him. The risk is that like Napoleon's marshals, the inferior talent may let down the Master. The main demerit of centralisation is that it may breed 'yes men' incapable of exercising independent judgment. This is serious because when 'the old man' passes on there may be no management left in the company. Ford built up a personally managed empire which nearly collapsed after his death. His grandson had to import managers from General Motors which had been managed in a totally different way. Sometimes an organisation has been built up in a most haphazard way and it is necessary to centralise in order to obtain some form of control over virtually independent satraps. Afterwards the inefficiencies of excessive control lead to a bout of 'pushing responsibility down the line', 'trusting the man on the spot', 'giving opportunities to emerging talent' and many other phrases.

The ideas tend to go in cycles. In the interwar years centralisation was more fashionable. Postwar the tendency has been towards decentralisation. More recently, the development of computers and other office machinery has created the belief, or the illusion, that greater central control is now more feasible. The managing director gets the monthly figures for the branch plant before the local manager, and is on the telephone to that luckless individual before he has had time to think up a satisfactory explanation. One reason advanced for the long survival of the Roman empire was their very poor communications, especially the absence of the cable and the telephone. The distant pro-consuls had been well soaked in the ethos of the empire by public service in Rome before appointment, and had to be trusted with the local administration. The old trading companies had to rely on the man on the spot as there was no way of controlling the day-to-day operations. One firm informed me that one of the hidden and unexpected benefits of establishing branch factories away from the parent was that the local managers could no longer keep running into their superiors' offices, and had to take their own decisions.

Another reason for organisational changes is that as a firm grows its organisation becomes inappropriate for its new problems. Concentration may be proceeding in one part of the company while decentralisation is the general rule. Different factories may be producing different end-products but based on a common expertise or technique. Each may undertake its own research. It may be decided to bring all this together in one central research establishment, or leave the departments intact and introduce some sort of device for co-ordinating the activities. One research department may be struggling with a problem which has either been solved or proved to be incapable of solution in another research department. A knowledge of this would save time and money for the company. It is also impossible to know where research will lead. A discovery in one part of a company may be set aside because it has no immediate bearing on its current work, yet this offshoot could be immensely valuable in another part of the organisation. The knowledge exists somewhere in the organisation but does not always get to the right people. I put this problem to a former employee in a research department of a very large firm which relied heavily on research for its new products, and asked him how this knowledge was co-ordinated and the short answer was that it wasn't, nothing was done. It was this sort of frustration in the work which made my informant a former employee.

It is this lack of certainty in organisational structure which provides opportunities for the consultant. It is almost certain that the organisation will contain excesses of one kind or another that call for correction. If there is overcorrection, there is the opportunity for another consultant at a later date to re-reorganise the reorganised company.

We can see this lack of finality in management structure by examining the history of the changes in some large-scale organisations.

The early railway companies were small, dealing with the problems of the traffic on a short stretch of line. In 1831 the directors of the Liverpool and Manchester Railway attempted to control the day-to-day management of the line down to the minutest detail. Later, committees were set up for various purposes and responsible salaried officials were appointed. A large railway operation, such as a main-line London terminus, can work only if thousands of men in different jobs are disciplined enough to do exactly as they are told. When they feel they have a grievance and 'work to rule' there is chaos.

As the railways increased in size they adopted the departmental method of organisation. Separate departments were set up and each officer down the line was responsible to his departmental superior. Co-ordination was effected only at the top, through the general manager. There were often conflicts of function at the operating level. The commercial department in an endeavour to gain traffic might make unreasonable demands on the operating department, and the latter might attempt to reduce costs of operation without allowing for the effects on the customers. Some companies tried the divisional form of organisation (like the self-contained army division) and traffic managers down the line had the function of co-ordinating the work of the different departments. With the creation of the four main-line companies in the 1921 Act, different methods of organisation were followed. The Great Western retained the departmental system; the LNER had a central staff for certain functions, but operations were on an area basis, largely following the pattern of the main companies absorbed, and based on their London termini; the LMSR, with its long lines of communication, organised the work on self-contained divisions, so that long-distance traffic passed from one division to another. Thus four railway companies found different ways of organising their business to meet their own specific problems.

The 1947 Transport Act brought these companies into one unit. The former companies were now managed by the Railway Executive, which was responsible to the British Transport Commission

– two new tiers in the management structure. 'That created problems of organisation which delayed for years essential post-war re-equipment. However able the Commission, it is very doubtful whether they could have moved faster, because their undertaking was so vast it could hardly be managed at all.'[5]

The four main-line companies were reorganised into six regions, each under a chief regional officer, reporting direct to the Railway Executive. In 1954 the BTC and the Railways Central Staff were made responsible for financial control and general policy. Functional responsibilities were passed down to the area boards which now became increasingly autonomous. Local traffic managers took over some of the decision-making functions formerly carried out at headquarters. Thus, while the object of nationalisation was to co-ordinate transport throughout the country, the only way in which it proved possible to manage such a vast undertaking was to break it up into the former constituent parts and to give each a large measure of local freedom! And so it goes on. Sir Stanley Raymond, who became chairman after a career in railways and was sacked by a political decision, stated that 'in twenty-one years in public transport, half my time has been devoted to reorganisation, acquisition, de-nationalisation, centralisation, decentralisation'.[6] There are certain well-known economic problems of railways throughout the world, but constantly changing their internal structure at the whim of politicians does little to solve them.

The National Coal Board, set up in 1946, had similar organisational problems to those that faced the railways. But whereas the latter had gradually evolved from a multitude of separate companies into larger units over the course of time, the administrative structure of the board was set up completely *ab initio*. Over nine hundred collieries, separate joint-stock companies, some very large public companies, others small, public or private, were brought under one control. The difficulties were aggravated by the fact that the owners were generally opposed to nationalisation on principle, and did not have the background experience of the new type of organisation structure. A managing director of a moderate-sized coal company, responsible for the conduct of the company business, would not fit in well halfway up (or down) an organisational hierarchy. The administrative units, the boards of directors, disappeared at once, and many of the experienced men left the industry.[7] (In the gas industry the large undertakings, company and municipal, were taken over as they stood with largely the same individuals. In many cases it was possible to carry on as before with only a slight change in the name and title on the office doors.)

The board first grouped the collieries into areas as the main management unit, and as this would mean too many areas reporting directly to the board, an intermediate level was introduced, the division. Thus there was the board, controlling eight divisions and these controlling forty-eight areas, and these controlling the collieries. The line of command was the board, the divisional board, the area general manager, the colliery manager. In general (there have been exceptions at different times) the Coal Board is functional, different members of the board being responsible for a particular function, such as production, marketing, finance, industrial relations, staff and scientific, and this is repeated, where appropriate, at each lower level.

The Coal Board in 1953 invited five prominent and experienced people under the chairmanship of Dr Fleck of ICI 'to consider the organisation of the National Coal Board and to make recommendations to the Board'. In 1955 the Fleck Report was made to the Coal Board which not only acted on it but published it and made it available to the general public, warts and all.

Fleck came to the conclusion that the main structure was sound – this would probably agree with the experience of the members in facing similar problems – and approved the principle of line and staff. (What is called staff could equally well be called a functional type of organisation.) The report pointed to the similarity of problems in all large-scale organisations, with the additional difficulty that the board operated in an extractive industry and had not the freedom of choice of a manufacturing company. (We are not arguing here whether an extractive industry, especially a contracting one, ought to be organised in this way. That was determined by Parliament. We are examining how the board tackled the problem that was given to it by the state.) The Fleck Committee did recommend certain changes, which the board carried out. It criticised the fact that the board's policies were not being carried out in the divisions and areas, due to the difficulty of new staff in making adjustments to a new organisation, and due to inertia, habit, or lack of staff. The board had not insisted on its policies being followed. It had controlled with a light touch and some divisions had taken advantage of this. The divisions often did not do what the board required. As a result of Fleck's report in 1955 the board issued a new general directive that:

> Policy decisions of the Board must be properly and promptly carried out, and control must be firm; in this all levels of management must play their part. Policies must be expressed fully, specifically and, where necessary, in detail. Each level of management must avoid interfering in the day-to-day work of the level of management below it, but should exercise control by means of modern management techniques, including the use of approved programmes, followed by periodical reports and reviews of progress.

This directive expresses the dilemma between exercising control allied with the policy of decentralising work down the line.

Since then, with the reduction in the number of collieries and the contraction of the industry, it has been necessary to reduce the administrative structure. The division has been abolished and the functions of the area extended. It is to be noted that all this concerns only the administrative arrangements for a board controlling a large industry; the actual production will start at the individual pits, where the mine manager, like the captain of a ship, has a heavy burden of responsibility.

Imperial Chemical Industries was able to supply a director experienced in organisational problems to advise the Coal Board (and staff many other inquiries), because it had gone through many internal changes itself. ICI was a merger of large companies in 1926 which had a significant share of the market in many chemical products, at a time when free trade was giving way to protection – 'it was conceived in monopoly and nurtured in protection'. As the amalgamation was brought about by strong personalities it is only to be expected that the early management was highly autocratic and personal. When the chairman got in the lift others got out. The directors had executive duties and approval for a course of action often had to wait for the sanction of the chairman.

In 1937 the organisation was decentralised. The chairman was freed from the taking of day-to-day decisions. This function was given to seven executive directors, each responsible for a section of the company's activities, and they formed a management board presided over by the chairman. A more fundamental reorganisation took place in 1943–4. The board was separated into four functions;

the chairman and four deputy chairmen were executive directors but without any specific functions. There were seven functional directors, covering the commercial, development, finance, overseas, personnel, research and technical areas. There were six operational directors, responsible for the operation of specific divisions of the company: heavy chemicals, dyestuffs and pharmaceuticals, ammonia and agriculture, metals, explosives, and paints and plastics. The fourth function was that of the outside or 'lay' directors, that they 'bring to the deliberations of the board a wealth of general outside commercial and industrial experience'. They are specialists of general ideas, and are ICI's justification for the use of non-executive outside directors. The numbers and the duties are those of 1944. At times there have been changes in the number of deputy chairmen, sometimes four and sometimes three, the grouping of functions has altered with changes in output and the functions have changed. But the principle has remained.

A fourth reorganisation came in 1963. It was more reminiscent of an army higher command. Each of three deputy chairmen had a general control of three liaison executive directors responsible, for example, for the dyestuffs, fibres and paints divisions. Under them is a divisional board for each product, under its chairman, who is not an ICI director but at the next lower level of management. Functional directors are retained, but with one very important change. In some cases the one director will have overall responsibility for an operating division, such as agriculture, and a functional responsibility for commercial; or for pharmaceuticals and personnel. In addition there are two field directors responsible for petrochemicals, and fibres and textiles, each of which also has an executive division. Attempts to reproduce this on an organisation chart, with all the interrelationships between functions and product activities, would require a three-dimensional model almost as complicated as the molecular structure of some of the company's products!

The first reaction to seeing this type of structure was of amazement. How can one director, trained as a chemist or engineer by profession, manage concurrently two such diverse activities as being responsible for, say, the production of plastics in a number of different factories, with that of the oversight of research and development throughout ICI? On closer inspection the logic is apparent: of course he cannot exercise the detailed function of management, so he *has* to delegate. The management of each division is in the hands of the divisional chairman and the management of each function will be controlled by a senior manager and his staff. Thus, more authority is delegated to the management while the directors exercise a wider range of interests concerning the company as a whole, which is what directors should be doing.

How this works in practice is impossible to know at the present. ICI has never had a major catastrophe such as many other firms have had, so that there has been no outside investigation by auditors or the government producing revealing and entertaining reports like those on Crichel Down, Aberfan or Pergamon Press. This is a negative measure of success. One occasionally hears rumblings from distant parts of the empire but ICI is able to wash any dirty linen it may have in private.

Unilever on the other hand offers much detailed information; its history has been well documented by Dr Charles Wilson. We saw how when Lever died the large number of diverse companies he had built up or acquired were in need of a strong control. The 1929 amalgamation of Lever Brothers with the Dutch Margarine Union to form the present Unilever imposed additional administrative management problems. Added to this were the problems imposed by the Great Depression.

At the top are two companies with identical boards, Unilever Ltd in Britain and Unilever NV in Holland. At the start there were thirty-two members, served by four secretaries, two from each group. Special meetings of the board were held in various European cities. This 'travelling circus' was a waste of time and full meetings were reduced to three a year and the management was transferred to smaller executive meetings of directors. Eventually D'Arcy Cooper (Lever's successor as chairman) won agreement for London to be the permanent headquarters as most of the directors worked there. Many of the Dutch had operated in London with large margarine sales through their subsidiary multiple shops.

A special committee of the board was formed in 1930 (thirty-two cannot manage) with eight members and this was gradually reduced to four. The whole organisation worked through a series of committees, at board level, lower down and further down. New headquarters had to be built to house the committees and the advisory departments – one of Professor Parkinson's danger signals![8] There were committees on everything; altogether there were forty-eight committees with over two hundred members. Some were on the committees to watch the others because of the early family mistrusts.

There was strong central control, essential to discover what was happening in a rather ramshackle empire, and to introduce some sort of order. With the shortage of money there had to be strong financial control and there had to be standardisation of accounting and salaries. But there were complaints that this control was excessive. According to a Canadian, one had to cable London before going to the bathroom. But it was clearly recognised that the main problem was one of communications, long before communications became a catchword in management jargon. The centre had to see that its policies were being carried out, and the distant, far-flung managers of shops, factories and plantations had to feel that their views were understood at the centre. This problem was tackled by directors and experts from headquarters travelling endlessly, reporting on factories and local conditions, and, most important, on men. For, Unilever believed, given the right man in the right job there was not much to worry about.

The problem was to find sufficient people of the right calibre to do jobs that did not exist in the smaller organisations and the company embarked on a policy of recruitment from both outside and inside the business of trainees to deal with the vast, complex problems. Unilever was one of the very few companies that had this sort of management recruitment and development policy before the war (others were department stores and some of the much-maligned colliery companies). It has since been imitated by many others.

During the Second World War many of the businesses were overrun by the enemy although they continued to function. Unilever discovered that although communications between the centre and the individual businesses had been broken, local managers lived up to their responsibilities. This strengthened the urge to a further decentralisation of the vast complex. A current organisation chart would show the familiar line and staff, the lines going down to the divisions and regional groups, and from there to the national managements in each country, and to the operating units. Advisory and service departments, accounts, finance, legal, personnel, and so on, provide the staff.

According to Lord Cole the business must delegate or bust. As the business world is changing all the time speed of decision is essential. There can be no speed if everything has to be laboriously referred up the rungs of the ladder to be mulled over and debated and a ruling given. What is worse, this would stifle management talent and initiative throughout the company. Each business operates with the minimum of control. There is, however, some control for without it there would be anarchy. The controls are of three kinds.

Annual operating plan Each unit makes an estimate of its sales, margins and expenses for the year. These have been discussed in detail with the regional group, with any advisory or service department that is necessary, and with the product co-ordinators. This is necessary because the plans of one Unilever unit can affect others in the group – it is no use two margarine factories in different countries planning to increase output by exporting to the other country. These individual plans are co-ordinated by the special committee of the board and when approved become the yardstick by which the unit's performance is measured.

Capital expenditure The units make similar plans for capital expenditure. Different amounts of capital expenditure may be approved at different levels in the organisation; it is only the major items which have to go to the board. As Unilever provides the capital there must obviously be some overall control.

Selection of top management Below the board there are about 200 senior managers upon whom the efficiency of the business depends. Lord Heyworth in 1949 stated that:

> The man on the spot must either be backed or removed. It is not sufficient to leave him there and overrule his decisions and recommendations. The man on the spot is bound to make a certain number of mistakes. It is necessary, therefore, to be sparing in reproof when he exceeds his authority, because initiative is a very tender plant whose growth must be fostered even if it involves a few weeds flourishing too.

These ideas have met with greater acceptance in recent years, although it cannot be said that large firms have solved the problem of the successful organisation of their work. Large organisations are broken down into smaller units so that each is a manageable unit in itself. The different ways are: first, by function, where all work of a similar nature is brought into one department. This is the functional method of organisation. Second, by area, where the emphasis is on the geographical distribution of the firm's activities.

If the separate plants are considered as separate businesses under the one overriding financial ownership, the management problem is less than if the whole is operated from the centre. Area boards in coal and electricity are examples of this method. Setting up separate companies for trading overseas is another version. Third, by factory, where different factories are set up in the same area, or more commonly in other areas. There are many examples of firms with a number of different factories producing the same goods instead of having all the production in one factory. Fourth, by process, where the emphasis is on the process of manufacture, and different processes are under separate management, such as car bodies and car engine manufacture. And fifth, by product, emphasising common elements in the product in a multi-product company, such as the distinction between heavy goods and domestic goods in a large electrical company, or fertilisers and drugs in ICI.

Large companies may put their trust in one form rather than another, and they may change their emphasis in the method of control. The forms of industrial structure are in a constant flux as managers seek new answers to their problems.

Notes

1 Xenophon, *Scripta Minora,* Loeb Classical Library, Heinemann, 1925, p. 47. This courting of short-period popularity with the 'lower orders' may help to explain the palace revolutions of the frustrated officials.
2 Sir Miles Thomas, *Out on a Wing,* p. 277. This is also a source of information on William Morris.
3 It is impossible not to sympathise with those struck down when the bloated organisation sheds its fat, especially when it is no fault of the victim. But some managers bring it upon themselves by empire building and prestige expansion. As Alaric told the trembling Romans, 'the thicker the stubble the more easily it is mown'.
4 Where some of this staff work is intermittent, i.e. is not required every day, it may be contracted out. Government departments administer a policy laid down by Parliament; when this policy is questioned, or is in need of a change, outside advice is obtained by the appointment of royal commissions, etc. Businessmen call in consultants for particular needs.
5 R. Kelf-Cohen, *Nationalisation in Britain,* Macmillan, 1961, p. 55.
6 Sir Stanley Raymond, *Sunday Times,* 7 January 1968.

7 At that time there was an advertisement for an experienced colliery manager overseas. More than 900 applications were received, equivalent to one from each colliery in Britain.
8 C. Northcote Parkinson, *Parkinson's Law*, John Murray, 1958.

Seven

The managers

> It is apparent from the accounts alone that a number of persons, wishing to batten on the estates of the Treasury, have invented titles for themselves, such as comptroller, secretary, or superintendent, whereby they procure no advantage to the Treasury but swallow up the profits.[1]
>
> Letter from Servaeus Africanus to the District Governor of Middle Egypt, A.D. 288

Who is the manager? Obviously he is the one who manages, and this raises the question of what is management? There is a difficulty of definition and different words in this field are used in many different ways, sometimes inclusive and sometimes exclusive. When the author first started on the long road to this inquiry he sat, among others, a degree paper on business organisation. Later he taught his students a subject known as business administration, and even later a subject termed business management, also known as management principles and practice. Allowing for slight changes in subject matter and differences in approach to suit examination requirements, the syllabus was the same in each case. So the words organisation, administration and management are interchangeable. Yet there is some difference between them.

When a firm is described as a 'well-managed company' this must obviously refer to its activity as a whole; it cannot mean that it has a perfectly run office organisation, keeping tidily the records of a factory that is producing the wrong goods at the wrong price. So 'managed' is used in the comprehensive sense of covering policy and execution. Yet it is usual to separate out the two parts of business success, the directors (or other heads) determining the policy, and the 'management' carrying it out. The word management is here used in a restrictive sense of putting into practice a predetermined policy, no matter how wise or foolish that policy may be. We can see this distinction clearly in the public sector, where the 'directors' are the Parliament, determining the policy through the Acts, and delegating the details to the minister who is a departmental managing director, and who works through the civil service. Here the detailed management comes from the administrative class at the top and the executive class lower down. At one time the civil service will be administering or managing a particular policy as laid down, and later with a change in government, the same people will be administering the opposite policy. The two aspects of the one factor of management are nicely separated. In business, the directors lay down the policy and the managers, production managers, sales managers and office managers, carry it out.

While this is quite clear in theory it is blurred in practice. The manner in which a policy is carried out is in itself the firm's policy in operation. The directors may lay down the policy that the customer is always right and must have prior consideration, but the employees who deal directly with the customers may adopt a totally different attitude. As far as the outsiders are concerned the firm's policy is one of indifference to their needs. A complainant may experience opposition from an employee, but a great deal of consideration if he can get his complaint dealt with at the owner-manager level. And the reverse may apply.

Second, the policy decisions taken at the top are partly determined by the executive. Orders flow down and information flows up. Proposals, briefs and suggestions are put up to the board to make decisions. It accepts these or rejects them. It may never have the opportunity to consider alternative possibilities. Direction and management in both policy matters and execution are inextricably mixed. This is quite evident where we have managing directors and executive directors with feet in both camps.

Would it perhaps be better if we used the word 'management' to cover the whole operation of the business, kept the word 'administration' for the actual 'running of the business' and retained execution for the function and executive for the functionary? But the use of manager for executive is too common to be changed now. It is a little confusing, but we use the word management to cover the whole operation, and manager to mean 'the non-policy-making executive'.

What does the manager (executive) do? According to Mr E. F. L. Brech in *Management: Its Nature and Significance* (Pitman, 1967), that which all managers have in common are subordinates who look to them for guidance in the performance of their jobs. The manager has to prepare and issue plans for the work, to set up standards of performance, to give decisions and issue instructions, and to supervise performance and results. Thus a production manager, a sales manager, or an office manager, all have staff in their departments for whom they are responsible, and have to control and administer these people. Irrespective of the specialised work done in each department there is a common element of management that applies to all.

It is this common element of management which has led people to draw comparisons with different institutions and, by analogy, to seek to improve a particular enterprise by drawing on the experience of others. Those with military experience point out how certain principles of army organisation can be applied in business; for example, the principles of the Military Staff College have been extended to the Administrative Staff College at Henley for the training of business staff. The reverse transfer of ideas is over two thousand years old, and goes back to Socrates.[2]

> 'Do you mean to say, Socrates, that the man who succeeds with a chorus will also succeed with an army?'
>
> 'I mean that, whatever a man controls, if he knows what he wants and can get it he will be a good controller, whether he controls a chorus, an estate, a city or an army.'
>
> 'Really Socrates,' cried Nicomachides, 'I would never have thought to hear you say that a good businessman would make a good general.'
>
> 'Come then, let us review the duties of each that we may know whether they are the same or different.' [What follows abandons the dialogue form.]
>
> It is the duty of both to make their subordinates willing and obedient.
>
> And to put the right man in the right place.
>
> Both should punish the bad and reward the good.
>
> Both will do well to win the goodwill of those under them.
>
> It is to the interest of both to attract allies and helpers.
>
> Both should be able to keep what they have got.
>
> Both should be strenuous and industrious in their own work.
>
> Both are bound to find enemies, and it is important to get the better of them.
>
> That is just where it will be most helpful (to the objection that business capacity is no help when it comes to fighting). For the good businessman, through his knowledge that nothing pays or profits like a victory in the field, and nothing is so

> unprofitable and entails such heavy loss as a defeat, will be eager to seek and furnish all aids to victory. . . . Don't look down on businessmen, Nicomachides. For the management of private concerns differs only in point of numbers from that of public affairs. Neither can be carried on without men, and the men employed in private and public transactions are the same . . . and those who understand how to employ them are successful directors of public and private concerns, and those who do not, fail in both.

An objection was made, when Nicomachides was able to get a word in, that although there are common elements, business and warfare are two different activities. Management cannot be separated from the activity managed. It is not like a spiritualist's ectoplasm, a vague, non-material substance floating round in the air. Some modern discussions of management appear to treat it as something in its own right, people 'go into management'. There is no abstract management, only something or someone that has to be managed. In the above example, the general is managing an army and the businessman a business, and although some of the qualifications necessary are the same in each, the medium through which these are exercised are distinct. There must be some knowledge of the problems and characteristics of the activity to be managed. We may call this the technical content of management. As the manager has to guide the subordinates in their job he must know something about the nature of the job. Managers who do not, make some awful howlers and excite derision among the people they are supposedly guiding. On the other hand, if he really does understand the job and is personally competent, say the captain of a ship or a mine manager, much is forgiven him for any other shortcomings. He must understand the nature of the craft if he is to issue instructions and check on performance. The amount of technical content varies with the nature of the task and the level of management.

Brech distinguishes three levels: top management: departmental, sectional or functional, and lower or supervision; and four elements of management: policy, co-ordination and motivation, planning and control, and supervision and day-to-day decisions on technology. These elements are applied in different amounts progressively. Top management is concerned mainly with policy, co-ordination and motivation and not with operational technology.

Middle management has a smaller policy element, and a smaller co-ordination but a much larger element of planning and control and the beginning of supervision. At lower or supervisory level, there is a small element of policy and of co-ordination, but much more of actual supervision and day-to-day decision-making on the particular technology employed. The word technology here means the conduct of the trade or craft, the work of a machine shop, organising a repair garage, allocating stock to retail counters, serving meals in a hotel, all of which require a knowledge and experience of the work to be done.

One of the barren controversies in this field is whether the foreman is to be regarded as a part of management. Foremen are concerned primarily with one aspect of management, at the main point of impact. They are seeing that the firm's policy is being carried out, they are issuing instructions and checking on performance. Their powers will depend on the nature of the work and on the management policy of the firm. In some cases he is 'the man on the spot' or the 'senior officer present' and much depends on him. In the more jobbing type of work his responsibilities for organising are greater. Where the policy is for more central control and the issue of detailed instructions, as with some of the applications of 'scientific management', he may be little more than a gang boss responsible for discipline and the flow of work, but even this is a part of the total management of the company.

Some would like to exclude him from the role of management as he is not part of the higher thinking. Perhaps this is because of the normally distinct social background. The foreman has come from the ranks and wears a white coat and is close to the noise and the dirt. He has not been specially recruited and earmarked for higher things and his educational background is different. But he is responsible for implementing the firm's policy, at the point where it is most important, and is carrying out a part, if only a limited part, of the total managerial function. But this limitation does not apply only to the foreman. It applies throughout the organisation, especially in large and complicated businesses. It is only in the small owner-manager businesses that one man, or a few co-partners, make all the bold decisions and hold all the management reins. The single, total element of management is performed by a large number of different people with the result that the actions of even the senior managers will be circumscribed and limited. Division of labour occurs in management as on the factory floor and the work and the functions are spread over many different people at higher and lower levels.

The French engineer, Henri Fayol (*General and Industrial Management*), lists six abilities which are a necessary part of the management: technical, commercial, financial, security, accounting and managerial. It is the last which is most probably meant when the word management is used (in its restrictive sense of administration) but the other five are part of the management of the firm in the sense of a successful and 'properly managed' company. In total, or business, management, he states that the technical is of great importance but probably overrated. It is less important at the top, or general management level and more important lower down. The commercial knowledge of buying and selling is as important as a knowledge of production. There must be an understanding of the market and of competitors and business contracts. Financial knowledge covers obtaining capital, making use of available funds and avoiding foolhardy commitments. Security is the safeguarding of property against theft, fire and flood. Accounting covers the present position and future trend and should be clear and simple. It is only the managerial, the selection and training of personnel, setting up the organisation, making decisions, instructing, planning and co-ordinating, which is normally covered in modern management.

The manager is concerned with one function out of six. He is doing a limited task but the efficiency of the company depends on the blend of all six. Some are implicit in the work carried out. The word 'technical' not only applies to the techniques of the industry, such as flour-milling or cotton-spinning, but to the techniques of the functions being performed. The personnel manager has his techniques of selection; the market research manager uses his sampling techniques; the transport manager has a technical expertise in the comparative costs and advantages of different methods of conveying the company's goods to their destination; the accountant has his knowledge of bookkeeping.

But generally managers will not be troubled with financial matters; the money they use is provided by the organisation. It is an external fact of life, and if not manna from heaven, it is provided for them free, though there is interdepartmental jockeying for a larger share of the free allocation. Many managers will not be concerned with commercial matters. The ultimate success of the company depends on selling at a price over cost but the production men are not bothered with sales and the salesmen with production costs. All the others in the management team are doing work which is relevant, or is thought to be relevant, to the operation of the organisation, but is not directly linked to the main commercial purpose.

The total unit of management is spread out and diffused over all the managers, specialists and executives. He is dealing with the individual tree and not the wood or the forest. The total management is like a jigsaw of different pieces that have to make up a complete picture. But unlike the jigsaw the pieces do not always fit together easily into a predetermined position. The specialist has three loyalties or objectives: to the firm, to the department, or to the profession. In the first case he may join a firm straight from school or university. He is 'with Universal Dealers' or 'something in World Products' with no particular trade or craft in mind. Later by accident or training he gravitates to one department or another, and if he finds it congenial, and if his employers find him competent, he becomes wedded to that part of the company's organisation. The important thing is that he looks to the company as his source of income, promotion and pension. He may move upwards by going sideways into a similar speciality. If a new department is established it may be staffed by people with a similar background of experience.

Within this general employment he may become highly specialised. He acquires by practice and theoretical study a deeper knowledge of this limited work. He is more and more immersed in the work of the department. There is the big world outside – not outside the company, which is a much more distant landscape, but the other departments and specialities which occasionally impinge on his own work. But his main activities and interests are in the field of his own speciality and there is a sense of common purpose with his fellow practitioners. They can talk to each other in the common jargon which excludes outsiders from participating in their ideas. Where there is a professional knowledge to be acquired and shown by examinations and qualifications the common bond is strengthened. Differences in rank are not differences in background, expertise, education or social position. The differences are time and maturity. The articled clerk is the chartered accountant of the future and the junior engineer will one day be a full member of the professional body. Outside the firm they will gather on a basis of equality – tinged by a certain deference to the elders of the tribe – at the meetings of their professional bodies. In times of difficulty such as the possibility of an encroachment on their particular functions, they will form squares at the approach of the cavalry or the Dervishes from the outer desert. Professional demarcation may be as strong as the fight to determine who bores the holes in a shipyard.

To a large extent the management expertise consists of a knowledge of the particular organisation's management structure, an understanding of where the tenuous lines of communication cross and re-cross each other, where authority lies, the workings of inter-departmental committees, and even a fine and exact sense of office politics. For many people who have risen in an organisation, one of their main strengths is this acquired knowledge which applies to that organisation only. They have a higher economic value in that organisation than in any other. But the professional man has a transferable skill, which may have an equal or higher value somewhere else. It just so happens that he is employed by A rather than B and if he does not like the way in which his career is going he can move fairly readily, sideways and upwards. This is particularly true where a specialised department or activity has acquired a reputation in the outside world. Engineers trained at XY are much sought after, in the estate agent's phrase, by other engineering companies, even although XY is not distinguished for its profitability. The reputation of Ford's costing and control system has meant an influx of ex-Ford men into companies with their own inadequate systems. Marks and Spencer managers are to be found in comparable companies. Local government 'professionals' and teachers move round as part of their normal career. This is assisted by the policy of employers throwing vacancies open to competition, and what they gain by bringing in outsiders they lose with the exodus of their own staff. It needs only one disappointed internal promotee to cause a mass migration of ambitious staff.

While this free movement of skilled labour helps to spread the existing scarce supply there are losses as well as gains. The acquired internal expertise concerning the particular organisation is lost. There is not the same loyalty to the institution. The sojourn there may be regarded as a necessary period in the wilderness in preparation for the promised land of a better job somewhere else. The footloose newcomer spends one year acquiring a knowledge of the job, he makes some contribution in the second year, and moves on in the third before his mistakes come to light. The head of one department where outside recruitment is normal, stated that he would never consider for interview a man who had served less than two years in his current post. He was tired of the procession of young men with no real interest in the job. On the other hand it is remarkable how some employers view the man who has performed exactly the same job with a number of different employers, as being more experienced than the man who has done the same, and had a more varied experience, within the one firm. The latter has at least stayed long enough for his chickens to come home to roost.

While the specialist function may exhibit a staff relationship within the organisation, there is a line relationship internal to that department. The head will have his assistant head and his assistant to the head; there will be sectional sub-departmental heads overseeing the work of others. The functional specialists are managers of their departments although they may not be termed 'management' in the sense of the general administrative management of the company. This term is usually retained for those in direct line management.

Many people at the top in industry are critical of the results of the increasing specialisation of function. The paradox is that to succeed in his calling a man must acquire an expertise in his particular profession. As he progresses his expertise becomes of lesser importance and he is called upon to exercise talents quite distinct from his profession, and for which he has had no training. Lord Chandos (then chairman of AEI) made this point very clearly in the 1962 Elbourne Memorial Lecture. He told the story of a young man who wished to be an engineer. He had to make up his mind whether to be a mechanical, a civil or an electrical engineer. He chose the third. Even within electrical engineering there are many specialities. The young man takes his degree and specialises in electronics and telecommunications. He enters the service of a large electrical company and by his ability and hard work gets promoted to assistant superintendent of a division of the company employing 1,500 people.[3]

> Almost overnight things start coming on his desk, in a painful manner, which have got nothing whatever to do with light current engineering, and still less to do with telecommunications. His boss has gone to the races, when the buzzer on his desk buzzes and the works manager says that 140 women on the assembly line refuse to continue work unless they are given

> another tea break. Unfortunately a knowledge of light current engineering will not readily provide him with the answer . . . His specialised training is probably a hindrance . . . the application of strict logic to human affairs is more often than not fatal to human relations.

Every superior, whether he is a man with responsibility for a department employing thousands, or a man-over-a-man relationship, is concerned with 'human relations' and this has nothing to do with technical expertise. Most learn by experience or analogy. They see how they have been treated by their superiors, and this attitude is passed on. Lord Robens stated that even years after nationalisation it was possible to appraise the prewar management of a colliery by the current attitudes of the employees. We have seen with our self-made entrepreneurs how some had an appalling record as employers, while others, because of a sense of justice or some attractive quirk in their character, excited admiration and affection.

The other complaint is that when people rise in their specialist function and reach top management they are unfitted by knowledge, training and temperament for the new responsibilities. The top management must see the firm as a whole and it must co-ordinate the specialities. In particular it must face financial decisions. Many directors cannot understand a balance sheet, and leave it to the accountant. Yet it is difficult to see how this can be otherwise. The departments are concerned with their own work, and they do not deal with the raising of capital, dividend policy, recruitment and promotion policies of the firm as a whole, general marketing or product diversification and acquisitions. If every manager in the organisation completely understood the company's balance sheet, including all the footnotes in the most obscure consolidated accounts, it would have no direct effect on his own work. A knowledge of exchange rates and international movements of funds affects only those who are concerned in these transactions. (Lord Chandos does point out that such knowledge is of great value to an engineer-salesman who is dealing with foreign customers, but the general principle applies.) In a large and complex organisation general commercial knowledge is of little relevance to the work of most managers.

It may be objected that every manager, and every employee as well, ought to realise that if costs rise, if sales fall off, if the company runs out of money, then their own jobs are in jeopardy. They ought to, and in their reflective moments they do know this. But it is still largely irrelevant to their own work. For most people direct saving of costs is not in their own interests. Where money is in issue they are spenders rather than savers. It is only where a department is completely separated and self-contained in all respects, including financial, such as in an independent subsidiary company, that there is the direct relationship between income, costs and results. Otherwise there is no measurement of effectiveness. If a department spends an additional £1,000, it does not matter. 'It is a big firm', and it is only a small part of the total turnover even if it is a larger proportion of the net profit.

We can apply the now fashionable cost-benefit analysis to this. Some expenditure by managers will benefit them directly but the costs are borne by the company. In the case of an individual he pays the costs of his own benefits. The contrast has often been made of the dual standard, of the expense-account lunch and the small suppertime snack at home. Compare the simplicity of William Morris's office at Cowley with the baronial splendour of many executive suites. One director of an expanding private company which was stuffed with spare cash from its own profits explained to me that 'we are content with small-powered cars', and on seeing them parked outside I almost believed that my own far from new car was an unjustified extravagance.

Honour makes up a great part of the reward of all honourable professions, as Adam Smith explained. It is a natural tendency of people to seek the regard, or avoid the positive disapproval, of their fellows, especially if they are in the same group. In employment the wage paid is only one of the factors determining the attraction of a particular occupation. The regard in which the office-holder is held is another. The self-made man goes about his scruffy office in shirt sleeves and mixes freely as there is no doubt as to his position. Diogenes could live in a tub and not the stockbroker belt and be respected by Alexander for his personal qualities. The brilliant research chemist's sports jacket shines out like a beacon among the executive blue suits. Those who are secure in their status can ignore the outward and visible signs if they possess the inward grace.

It is otherwise in the large organisation. Titles and the trappings of office are as important in modern business and administration as they were in the ancient empires. As they are part of the pay and an incentive to promotion they may be regarded as serving an economic function. Or they may be thought of as a cost imposed on the organisation by human vanity. The titles in themselves do not cost more money than that spent on painting the names on the doors. Everybody is a manager now, or an assistant, or a potential. (The professional man who is head of a local authority's administration is secure enough to be the Town Clerk.) The title of director has come down from its true meaning to cover departmental heads.

One of the visible signs of having risen in the world is having it made perfectly clear that others have not risen. Status depends on differences and not on an equality between all. One of the ways in which this is made manifest is by the conferment on the upper ranks of privileges which are not available to the lower. Otherwise they cease to be privileges. Rank also implies its obligations. The fact that a manager does not have to clock in is not to be taken as a licence to reduce his hours of work. On the contrary, when there is pressure of work he is expected not to clock off when the others go home. The provision of company transport has the economic function of saving the time of executives which is expensive to the company. A motor pool of cars, available for the company's business, is part of the transport system.

It may be that the time of the major directors is so important, and they have to be freed from minor worries so as to be able to concentrate their minds on the epoch-making decisions, that the supply of a chauffeur-driven quality car saves the company money. After all, the company does not want the chairman to make the wrong bid for a rival, or have a purge in the middle management, because he got frustrated in a traffic jam or because he could not start his own car that morning.

But the supply of a car to various executives who do not use them for the company's business is only economic in the sense that it entails a privilege and is a part of the total emoluments. If not given some other form of payment, an even higher salary would be needed to attract and keep the right executives. One wonders what would be the result if instead of a company car employees had a cash option, as was the case with the old navy rum ration!

In the civil service the knowledgeable can tell the rank and pay of a man by seeing the size of the office, the type of desk and the type and size of carpet. In industry the line between the top and the ordinary workers is drawn by similar means. The civil service works to set rules and this imposes some restraint but there is no limit to the magnificence in large companies. A large area of desk space containing nothing but an unused blotter and a battery of telephones; the hierarchy of desk sizes getting smaller and more loaded with paper; the botanical specimens, with the rubber plant being the status favourite; the clothes closet, the hat stand, the set of pegs and the nail on the wall; the silver tea service, the Wedgwood china, private tea-making by the secretary, the ration tea brought round on the trolley; all of these compare unfavourably with the functional austerity that the author has seen in the directors' offices of successful private companies.

In the latter case the directors are spending their own money and in the former they are managers of other people's money rather than of their own and the expenditure is not viewed with the same anxious vigilance. It is certainly not suggested that directors and senior executives deliberately waste the shareholders' money. But it is suggested that in many details of the work the interests of the individual are opposed to the interests of the company. Status depends partly on the number of people in the department so it is in a man's private interest to add to his staff, while it is in the firm's interest that the work be done with as few people as possible. The man who suggests some cost saving on the factory floor is regarded as a bright prospect and is allowed to eat in a more senior dining room. The man who suggests that many thousands of pounds would be saved by abolishing the 'charity wagons', as the lower echelons see them, and having a small pool of cars available, or even to make an arrangement with a local taxi firm, would be shunned by his peers and have to eat alone.

It is interesting to see how the pattern of expenditure overflows into private life. It used to be said, in the days when expenditure was largely in the form of personal services rather than on physical goods, that every extra thousand a year a man acquired was one more person upon whom he was dependent. Now promotion means that there are greater commitments clawing at the increased salary. Surveys have shown that when people are promoted there is a tendency to move to a better house. Every step up the ladder means an increase in the mortgage. The two-car garage is no longer sufficient. There must be a boat, even if the owner is seasick, tied alongside the jetty. Promotion instead of leading to ease and comfort can be a step towards financial anxiety. Many a young man climbing the executive ladder incurs expenditure beyond his present means on the expectation that, with promotion, future increases in income will cover the debts. But as the manager's life is fraught with much uncertainty, especially among the older men, there appears to be a lack of wisdom in this attitude. This is how they manage their own affairs; how do they manage other people's?

The supply of managers

Every age has its economic problems. In the interwar years one of the main problems was adjusting the business economy to the after-effects of the war; to make profits with some of the major industries declining, especially those dependent on exports. Generally we could say that these problems were the problems of competitive business. Since the Second World War the emphasis has changed. The happy inflation has floated off the large amount of prewar unemployment, and this, together with the increase in world trade (compared with its collapse in the 1920s and 1930s), has made business conditions much easier. But another factor which is relevant to our problem here is the larger number of big businesses which have arisen, partly by natural growth but mainly by takeovers and amalgamations. So, one of the besetting problems of modern industry has been to acquire, train and retain sufficient people to staff the large corporations.

There always has been the problem of getting suitable people, such as the age-old problem of finding the just steward. The competent self-made entrepreneur complains that he cannot get employees with his own ability, forgetting that if they had his ability and ambition they would want to work not for him but for themselves. There is the exception – the man who does not want to take the risks himself, a first-rate foil for the rising entrepreneur. Boulton and Watt had an excellent and faithful foreman, virtually an assistant managing director, in Murdoch, and the Stephensons built the early railways with gangs of Geordies whom they knew and trained. Some second-rank men have risen by hanging on to the tail of the comet because they have the qualities necessary for this role. In general, however, it is true that the moderate-sized family business did not have the problem of getting managers that appears to be so intractable today. The top management was provided by family members and the intermediate management by clerks and foremen, often on a hereditary basis.

The 'problem', if it was thought of as such, was left to natural selection. Boys left school and got jobs. In some trade an apprenticeship was necessary. The universities were reserved for those following the learned professions such as law, medicine or theology, or as finishing schools for the sons of the rich whose function would be to administer the family estates. Those who showed promise at work could be promoted by the employers, for the lads came under the master's eye and their qualities could be assessed. In spite of what the present generation would consider a lack of educational opportunities, there were means available for the ambitious to acquire knowledge. The medieval system of apprenticeship survived in the articled clerk in the accountant's office and similar occupations, where a young man gained practical experience but was expected to pursue his professional studies in his own time. Industry and the professions could recruit from the more promising of the school-leavers at the age of sixteen or so. Older than sixteen was usually considered too old.

Employers were able to draw on a cross-section of potential ability and intelligence from the fourteen- to sixteen-year-old school-leavers. Banks did not specifically recruit boys of sixteen to be bank managers; they recruited clerks, the best of whom would rise to become managers. The position has now changed radically. The educational opportunities, with the postwar creaming off through eleven-plus, grammar schools, scholarships and universities, have produced many more people than are necessary to fill academic positions and certain of the learned professions. For those who follow the accepted path it is easier to obtain academic qualifications. For those who for various reasons do not go through the normal channels, it is probably more difficult to acquire qualifications on the 'self-help' principle. Previously people chose to acquire their qualifications in traditional professions such as accounting, engineering or law; now the tendency is towards more general academic qualifications, and choosing which career to enter afterwards.

The employers, and large firms in particular, have turned to graduates to fill the ranks of the middle and upper management. It is unlikely that this is caused by a sudden belief in the virtues of higher education. It is more likely that the people they want have escaped the sixteen-year-old net and have to be caught by a finer mesh at a later age. They do not recruit graduates as such, they recruit the people they need, and these recruits 'happen to have a degree'. The fact that by the year 2000 all managers will have a degree does not necessarily prove that that is the best qualification for business management. If discus throwing were a compulsory school subject, eventually all managers would be discus throwers. No doubt in their after-dinner speeches and in their memoirs they would attribute their success in life to the virtues of discus throwing, the discipline of training, the encouragement of the competitive urge, the physical build-up of brain and muscle co-ordination, and whatever other rationalisation struck them at the time.

Before the war only a few firms, for example Unilever and Lewis's, had a definite policy of graduate recruitment, but the general view was that the graduate was at no disadvantage if he kept quiet about his degree, and if he worked hard he might catch up with the early school-leaver who had by now five years' business experience.

Today the problem of selection is much greater. If a firm engages a hundred clerks with school certificate it might be satisfied if ten of them occupied junior managerial positions in five to ten years' time, and one or two were in a senior position by the time they were forty. The other ninety would find their own level in the organisation. If it now recruits ninety boys of lower average ability for the routine tasks, and ten older men as potential managers, it must make the right selection to provide the same number of managers. If the firm anticipates a 50 per cent fallout, it will recruit twenty for the ten future vacancies. The ten who do not make the grade have been educated and trained for a particular career and expectations which they do not realise. They may find success in other businesses or have to choose some other occupation. Many firms with what is called an enlightened policy of graduate recruitment experience a high labour turnover. The fallout may be much more than 50 per cent and companies may recruit a large number of graduates with executive potential and find that none of them remains after five years.

One difficulty to be met, especially where the graduate programme is a matter of fashion rather than of intellectual conviction, is that the firm does not know what to do with the trainees it has acquired. Under the old method, employees gained their experience and knowledge of the company by doing simple, routine jobs in keeping with their age and education. The office boy's job cannot be done happily by educated older men. Having solved all the pressing problems of the world in theory, and having been exposed to intellectual influences during a three-year course, graduates expect their work to be more interesting and demanding than this. Yet, whatever their potential, they have not the practical knowledge and experience of the company or business in general to be entrusted with the interesting jobs, those that carry responsibility and could cost the firm money.

A common solution is the 'Cook's Tour' where the graduate is passed from department to department to acquire a knowledge of the firm. He finds the process boring because he has nothing to do but 'watch Nelly' and the department find him a thundering nuisance and an interruption to their work – and the departmental executive who has served the firm from boyhood regards the trainee as a privileged competitor. Many graduates find this a complete let-down and leave. This applies less to people with technical qualifications where the trainee can be gainfully employed in the department. Close supervision may be necessary because of the gap between theoretical knowledge and the practicalities of industrial life. Some firms, such as Ford, have progressed from the idea of a two-year introduction followed by finding a regular job for the newcomer, to the principle of engaging graduates for specific tasks and putting them in those departments from the outset.

The principle, or the rationalisation, behind this policy is that of the benefit of the well-trained mind which can be applied to the problems of the organisation. It is true that there is a great demand for the exceptional 'double-first' in industry, the civil service and the professions, but it is less clear in the case of the ordinary pass-degree man, or similarly professionally qualified. Each has acquired a specialist knowledge in his own subject, but it does not follow that this has given him a transferable skill suitable for business administration. In fact it is recognised that at the degree qualification level people have different natural abilities and weaknesses. A man with a gift for languages may be hopeless at elementary mathematics and a good scientist may never be an expert in languages, including his own. Yet it appears to be assumed that the possession of a degree, in whatever subject, is evidence of a natural ability which can be applied to the commercial and personal problems of a business and administrative career. The possession of particular skills or training may, on the contrary, show abilities or traits which are a positive bar to such success.

This attitude can be seen in the requirements of certain courses which are designed for future managers. A man with any degree in any subject is automatically qualified for the course. A man who left school at sixteen and has by his own efforts of part-time study acquired non-graduate qualifications and considerable experience, has to prove his potential capacity for admission. The man with proved experience and nothing else has a very slender chance of being accepted as a 'special case'.

One may question this idea that knowledge of one field is particularly useful for work in a different field, especially in that of business management. It certainly does not apply in other callings. Hobbs and Sutcliffe were never denied the opportunity of opening for England because they did not have five 'O' levels, nor would one refuse to listen to Menuhin if it were announced that he had no 'A' levels, nor question a brilliant surgeon's knowledge of foreign languages before allowing him to remove an appendix. Such matters are completely irrelevant to the skills employed.

In fact brilliance in one field of activity may be accompanied by ignorance or stupidity in others. No one is more conscious of this than the professional economist, where the pronouncements of top scientists, publicists, and even businessmen, give him a sense of despair about the future. He may wonder how other professional men feel about the educated guesses of others about their own specialities. The 'trained mind' has to be trained in the subject to be applied.

Some of the postwar emphasis on the training for managers may have the contrary effect of reducing the supply. A rigid insistence on particular types of qualifications cuts off those who do not have these arbitrarily defined requirements. Able men may be condemned to the lower ranks. People who would have gone into industry or commerce from school go to a university instead, and as a result of new vistas opened to them seek other occupations. This tendency may be strengthened by an anti-business attitude in some schools and universities. The training may even disqualify them from a potential business career. Sir Paul Chambers has been highly critical of some of the university products.

The length of the career

A postwar feature has been the shortening of the managerial career. In the smaller business community the boy who was capable progressed in the firm, obtained a position of responsibility and importance, and eventually went to honourable retirement with the firm's blessing and a gold watch. He had a long career as an employee and as a manager. Now he starts later, rises quicker up to a certain point and may then get stuck. In the normal pyramidal structure of the large corporation there are many more posts at junior and middle management level than there are at the top. This is true of other organisations as well, such as the army and the navy. The captains outnumber the colonels. This could mean the lower ranks being staffed with elderly and experienced officers when the services want them young. The solution is the automatic cut-off. Promotion is normally certain and automatic up to a certain point, say to captain or major. Those who are not considered suitable for the very different requirements of the higher command are retired on pension. They either live on their pensions or have to seek some other occupation. The system was eminently suitable for men of private means or an inheritance to look forward to, who were not seeking a permanent career. The work span is even shorter in occupations depending on physical fitness. The professional footballer hopes to retire at about thirty and become the tenant of a pub near the ground which has been the scene of his triumphs. Such an occupational distribution requires that there are other occupations able to take the older people from the youth occupations. It also depends on the numbers. The number of majors and ex-centre-forwards is not too great to be absorbed. The case is different if the managerial career is very much shortened because the numbers are so large and the alternative opportunities so less evident.

In most large corporations there has been an increase in insecurity. There are many more managers. When something goes wrong it is the management heads that roll. Takeovers are normally accompanied by a massacre of the defeated. This may be partly the managers' own fault. If they had not been prone to empire-building and the enlargement of office there would not have been the scope for the hatchet man. If the new managing director can go into an office and instruct his assistant that he wants to be rid of half the people in that block; and if it does not matter which half, and if the work is still done or the unnecessary work is no longer done, this does not give that work undertaken before the purge a very high value. If the managers had done their own pruning, including that of items which add to prestige and expense, there would have been no scope for the takeover bidder to do the job. If the company's profitability had been greater he might not have had the opportunity.

Some senior management may be parasitical on society in this respect. They may expect their middle management to be zealous and hard working, putting the company before all others, and when the latter have worked themselves into ulcers and the fire of youth has departed, they are discarded in favour of the new batch of management trainees. Too young at twenty because of the training period, and too old at forty results in a working management career of twenty years, less than that of many professional cricketers. Yet in some of the professions, where knowledge and acquired skill are considered valuable, a man is just starting to prove himself in middle age. It is understandable that in a career which depends on physical prowess, strength and muscular co-ordination the earning period should be short; it is less evident that this should be so in occupations which are supposed to depend on judgment and the well-trained mind.

One alternative to the scrap heap would be for the trained and experienced manager to go into business on his own account. A few years ago it was reported that an association of redundant executives had been formed. Between them they must have covered all the specialities and skills of modern business. Few of them started a business. None of them got all the others together into some new enterprise. Nearly all waited for employment. This shows the essential difference between the attitudes and the qualities necessary for success in the large managerial corporation and those which make the entrepreneur or the businessman.

Early enforced retirement affects the supply of managers. The young man can see what is happening to his elders. It is no good the recruitment circus coming round to the universities to attract the best brains when it is obvious how some of these firms are treating their existing employees. It is no good offering prospects of early promotion if the far-sighted man can see that the next generation of entrants can be offered the same opportunities only at his expense, once he has been wrung dry. The policies and antics of some of the managerial leaders do little to command respect or loyalty from their staff. In both the USA and Britain many university students are prejudiced against a business career. This is partly due to ignorance of business among academics but a great deal of the blame must go to the dissatisfied within the business world who do little to attract recruits. So we have the paradox. On the one hand the inadequate supply of future managers, and on the other, the vast numbers of existing managers who are surplus.

It is argued that this pruning process is necessary to maintain the quality and efficiency of management. This will be the subject of the next chapter.

Notes

1 British Museum Papyrus 752.
2 Xenophon, *Memorabilia,* Loeb Classical Library, Heinemann, 1923, III, iv.
3 Viscount Chandos, 'General management in a specialist's world', *Manager,* December 1963.

Eight

The efficiency of management

> Large and complex industrial organisations have the problem of establishing 'professional management' and the use of modern techniques, while retaining the entrepreneurial drive for profit which is the mainspring of successful business.
>
> Sir Joseph Latham, *Take-Over. The Facts and Myths of the GEC/AEI Battle*

The justification for the periodic reorganisations, staff adjustments, introduction of new techniques, and the calling in of consultants is to increase the efficiency of the management. This implies that we know what management efficiency is and that we can recognise it when we see it. This could mean that there is some numerical measure that we can use, such as the firm is 85·7 efficient, or some ordinal test, that policy A is more efficient than policy B without being able to put a figure to it. While there is no absolute definition of good management, like the definition of absolute zero in temperature, there is a sense in which managements can be put in an order of merit. Some of the techniques in use attempt to answer this difficulty.

Economic theory has one answer to the problem. In the theory of competition, each firm uses up some of the scarce resources of the community for which it has to pay the market price – the current rate of wages, the ruling rate of interest on capital, etc. Its total costs represent the demands the firm has made on the community for the resources it has utilised. The management of the firm combines these factors of production in various ways to produce a product, whether it be an article or a service, for sale to the public. The firm's income is the price received for each multiplied by the number of units sold. The total receipts, or the gross income, represent the value that the community places on the firm's output. If sales value exceeds the costs the firm has used the scarce resources of the community in such a way that the community values the goods produced higher than the cost of producing those goods. If the value of goods produced is less than the cost of producing them, there has been a waste of scarce resources which could have been put to better use in some other way.

So the profit (or loss) is one measure of the firm's efficiency in satisfying the wants of the consumers. If the latter are willing to pay the cost of producing the product in the purchase price the firm is 'efficient'. If a firm has lower costs than its competitors it makes a larger profit and can expand by ploughing back profits. If it makes less, and if it does not cover its costs in the long run it is economically inefficient and goes out of business. It sets free its resources to be used by another entrepreneur.

This theory of the market says nothing about the efficiency of the managers or of the managerial techniques applied. The economic system exists to satisfy the wants of the consumers; the profitable firm does so therefore it is efficient. If tastes change the consumers will want different commodities. Those firms which adapt themselves to the new conditions will prosper. Those firms which do not will fail.

The theory of the market has to be modified in two directions. If a firm is a sole supplier of an economic commodity it may make more than average profits. Economic theory allows for this in the theory of monopoly, and attributes part of the profit to monopoly. But there is no way in which the firm's profit may be divided into business profit, which is normal, and monopoly profit. In the public utility field it has been impossible to measure efficiency and to state that a certain firm 'ought' to be allowed a certain amount of profit because it is efficient. If a firm has a monopoly there is no standard of comparison. Apart from that, it is too readily apparent that it is possible for the monopolist to incur losses if the market turns against the commodity. It is useless to acquire the monopoly of a product which is superseded by a new invention.

A second limitation to this theory is that a firm derives income for its own use but may be able to transfer part of the costs to the rest of the community, i.e. building a glue factory in a residential district reduces the value of the houses within windshot. Or a firm may benefit the community without being able to share costs. Discussions of pollution are currently fashionable, and the principles of these modifications to the normal competitive theory are well known to readers of Pigou's classic.[1] While these points must not be overlooked it is remarkable how often when a firm or an industry becomes unprofitable, it acquires an aura of respectability; it satisfies some deep social need; it becomes a basic industry; and is a public service. This is particularly so if the industry's difficulties are precisely because the consumers have found some other product or method of spending their money and have deserted the basic essential of life. Where profits are suspect it appears that only loss-making is respectable and has some deep civilising effect.

This general theory assumes that a firm is producing a product which it sells in the market in competition with similar products. The firm may have a number of different factories in different parts of the country producing one type of article. Here is an obvious measure of efficiency; the costs of the different factories can be compared and the laggards brought up to scratch.[2] Furthermore, many firms produce a great variety of products. While the profitability of the firm is apparent it is much more difficult to know the profitability or otherwise of the different products.

The other problem, particularly in the large firm, is to evaluate the efficiency of the thousands of different operations within the firm. In the case of a watch, if one wheel is removed the whole thing stops so no one part is more important than another. In the case of a rowing eight all men row at the same speed although some are more powerful than others. In the first case all operations are interdependent and essential, and in the second all work is co-operative and exactly the same as in a tug-of-war or cable-laying team. But where people are doing different work, how does one measure, or even guess at, the efficiency of, say, the costing department, the recruitment policy or the research expenditure?

It is sad and unjust that the efficiency or otherwise of such factors as mentioned above may be irrelevant to the success of the business. The important factor is the survival or profitability of the business as a whole, and the rest may or may not contribute to this end. But the two, business success and internal efficiency, are often confused, both in prosperity and failure. A company by accident or design hits upon a new product which cannot fail to sell at a price well above its costs of production. In building a new factory it strikes a gusher of oil which adds to its uncovenanted income. A huge profit is made. The company is successful in the economic sense of satisfying a market. But more follows. Its managing director is head of a successful company. He *must* be good to be in this position. He is an authority on business management. He is consulted on national issues and appears on the same television programmes as the secretary of the TUC. Whatever he does is the cause of the firm's success. If he takes all the decisions himself and trusts no one else to do a job without supervision, this is the future course of British industry. It extends further. Others acquire the reputation and the glory. The company sales director can address the annual conference of his professional association and explain how their own skilled management was the cause of the outstanding success. Commentators will extol the virtues of the costing system which contributes to the high profit, or if there is no such system, how the superior management of the company is able to dispense with such minor managerial aids.

It works in reverse. When down, kick hard. A firm may be in a contracting industry. It cannot help but make considerable losses. Nobody holds up its production control system as a model for the rest of industry,[3] or its office organisation as one of the best in the country. Yet the separate parts of the contracting firm may be more efficiently run than the same departments in another firm which is enjoying good fortune. There is a reason why this should be so. Where the profits are easy there is no incentive to look closely at costs and where the market is contracting there is a very strong incentive to get the costs down.

One difficulty about evaluating the efficiency of management is that, unlike the parts of the watch or the combined efforts of the rowing eight, much of what is done is useful but not essential. Tasks can be left unfulfilled without causing the organisation to collapse. The mixture and the size of the departments within the organisation varies greatly from firm to firm. Some companies have central service departments which hope to assist line management; other companies will not tolerate them.

Different departments, in spite of apparent similarities, get different results. The management principles of Marks and Spencer are well known. Marks and Spencer managers have a high transfer value in obtaining employment with other companies; the same people are doing the same job, yet the end result is different.

Three management problems

The problem of managing organisations can be split into three, which may be called Manad, Mancom and Mandec, if one wishes to join in the fashionable habit of providing new names for old problems.

1 *Manad* is the administrative aspect of management. It is the regular administration of a routine job. The same tasks are being

performed daily, weekly and annually. There is a proper routine which, if followed, will enable the tasks to be accomplished. Although there may exist a large measure of technical expertise in the particular activity, the work may be broken down by division of labour into its component parts and may present no particular management difficulty. The main thing is to prevent errors or breakdowns. One example is an examining body, such as that controlling the University of London GCE examinations. The organisation has to provide for the setting of the papers, the arrangement of the dates, the registration of the candidates, the distribution of the papers to the various centres in the country and overseas, the arrangements for the completed scripts to be sent to the appropriate examiners either directly or through the university, and for the results to be processed through the system and the schools and candidates informed. The system works and errors are few.

A similar routine organisation would apply to a gas company, or local authority department for example before the war. The industry was an established one. There was a system of meter readers making quarterly visits to the consumers' premises and reading the meters, or collecting the money from slot meters. The accounts were calculated and the bills sent out. Money was collected and reminders sent out to slow payers. With continuous reading the wheels turned on and on and the system worked. On the production side, the system of carbonising coal was well known and as retorts wore out they could be replaced by others of similar capacity. The complicated activity of operating a main-line terminus has been reduced to a routine, covered by a rule book designed to guide action in a variety of circumstances.

Such systems work in the sense that the particular job is done. Whether it could be done better or more cheaply is a different story. In some cases comparisons can be made with similar activities. Two gas or electricity local boards of the same size may have very different numbers of staff to service the undertaking. Or, if a unit of thirty people dealt with x customers, it would be an increase in efficiency if the same work could be done by twenty-five people. Such comparisons can be made only if the quality of the service is the same. Costs can be reduced by contracting the service provided until one reaches the ultimate absurdity of self-service in a service industry.

2 *Mancom* This emphasises the commercial aspect of manage-

ment. The objective is to supply a market with a product that the consumer is willing to pay for, and to be able to adapt the organisation to changes in market or supply conditions. The profitability of the operations is the objective test. This has nothing to do with administrative ability, or the lack of it. Administration is now a means to an end, and not, as is at times the case with Manad, an end in itself. In the large firm, with the separation of functions among different executives, the direct causal link between individual action and the profitability of the firm is broken. Some companies try to solve this problem by splitting up the business into 'profit centres' so that profits or losses may be attributable to particular sections. But so many of the departments are not concerned with direct trading that it is impossible to apply this principle throughout.

3 *Mandec* This aspect of management is less concerned with routine administration, and the emphasis is on decision-making. Of course there is an element of decision-making in the most routine activities, and in commercial management managers must decide on prices, numbers to produce, how to deal with customers, and so on. Mandec, however, is the section which takes the major policy decisions, not those which arise in the day-to-day operations. Every time an operator decides to press a switch, he is taking a decision. These oft-repeated decisions become daily routine. There is a different type of decision, which is in many cases a 'one-off' decision. It occurs once in the history of the business and is such that the firm has no previous experience to guide it. This covers the major policy-making activity of the firm and may make or break it. A firm decides that it will attempt to expand faster than its retained profits allow. This means large-scale borrowing or an issue of capital. If the latter, few accountants will have had actual experience of a share capital issue although it is standard textbook knowledge. So the work is usually put out to a specialist to whom it is a mere matter of routine.

A good example of the difference between routine and decision management occurred in the gas industry. It had settled down into a routine when North Sea gas was discovered. This did not mean the slow building up of a new product but the immediate conversion of apparatus in whole areas at one time. This was a once-for-all operation that had to be learnt.[4] Once experience has been gained in one area it can be used in conversions in other areas. It is unfortunate that once a body of knowledge and experience has been built up and all conversions made the knowledge becomes useless.

Another example was the GCE examinations. The elaborate system set up by the university to handle the flow of material broke down when there was a postal strike. It had to improvise other methods of distribution. The important point was to prevent delay in the publication of results as these affect the autumn intake of colleges and universities. The task was accomplished with very little delay. The university had had some previous experience in coping with railway strikes or threats of strikes, which always seem to loom up at the peak examination periods.

One definition of efficiency of routine management would be the absence of inefficiency. If nothing goes wrong the management is doing its job – at a price. The errors and inefficiencies that occur are so obvious. Examples are the letter which says 'statement enclosed' and it is not; the letter which is not answered; the letter which answers a different question from the one asked and when this is pointed out, the later reply blandly ignores the points made.

Then there is the inability to do anything on time. This varies from the plumber or repair man who says he will be around in the morning, but omits to state which morning of which week; or the shop which says call again on Wednesday, there will be some new stock in then; right up to the ship which takes a year longer in building than planned, and the long delays in completing factories, industrial installations and roads. It would appear that the word 'time' has no meaning and any statement which uses it is a pure fiction and has no reference to the Trades Description Act.

There is a peculiar way in which errors intensify. One may have pleasant and fruitful relations with an organisation, but if anything goes wrong, all seems to go wrong at once. It appears that any attempt to correct a mistake in a normally smooth-running firm causes such confusion that nothing which is done ever puts matters right. One way of keeping the customer at bay is to have only one telephone line to the service department and keep it in constant use.

Measuring efficiency

It is difficult to apply the economic test of efficiency in the large corporation. There are a number of ways in which some estimate may be formed, but all of them are less exact than the classical profit or loss, success or bankruptcy model. The assumption of profit-making might not be valid.

Broadly, we can measure the success of any undertaking against its objectives. What does it want to do, and how successful is it? What it does is to ultilise various means towards the achievement of some end. 'The end of medical science is health; of military science, victory; of economic science, wealth' is a statement which would be familiar to anyone who had got as far as the first page of Aristotle's *Ethics.* It is a sad reflection on the present state of the art of management that this statement of the obvious, that human activity is directed towards some end, is now elevated into a new technique of management, 'Management by objectives' – how else can management be judged?

There are many non-profit-making activities (not to be confused with loss-making businesses) where the profit motive is inappropriate. These have still to be managed, and as we have seen organisations such as the army, the church and the state have contributed to the pool of knowledge regarding human institutions. This pool is not wholly useless in business studies. In war, the efficiency is comparative. No matter how skilful the armies, both sides cannot win – some authorities aver that both sides tend to lose. The winning side always looks good and well managed and the loser appears to have defects in its operations. Morale is recognised to be important. At Corunna the retreating army was a rabble until it heard the enemy guns, and then it turned and formed ranks without having to be ordered. A losing eight is always more exhausted than the winners, although it has covered the same course at a lesser speed. But a heavily outnumbered and beaten army is recognised as not necessarily inefficient.

But as generals are as loquacious as politicians and are much given to memoir writing, we are made aware of vast inefficiency in the conduct of military campaigns. It seems to be easier to detect this inefficiency amongst one's allies and friends (especially if they are in a rival branch of the service) than it is to see this in the enemy. Businessmen in their less frequent memoirs paint a much rosier picture of human endeavour.

The management literature uses the church as an example of certain administrative principles, and the church has contributed the word hierarchical to this literature. How does one judge the efficiency of this form of organisation? In a salvationist religion it will be necessary to wait until the day of judgment for the member to know whether or not he has chosen the right policy or the right organisation. On an earthly level, critics have complained that the excessive span of control and the lack of supervision has meant that the real 'policy' has not been carried out. There have been periods in history when even the friends of the church have regarded it as a failure. It has tended to contract by schisms and breakaway movements. Its 'market share' has fallen in face of the competition from the younger firm operating from Arabia.

The statements that 'the end of economic science is wealth' and that 'businesses are conducted with a view to profit' require some qualification. This is generally true of the owner-managed business, but it does not mean that the objective is the maximum wealth possible. A 'reasonable income', some security for the future, a place in society, may be better than striving for even greater wealth. A man who makes half a million in business has not failed to make a million, unless that had been his objective. If he is satisfied with his goal he has succeeded in his objective.

The 'profit motive' is even less important in the larger corporation. Where directors have a small shareholding only, their income arises from fees, salaries, and expenses and even a large increase in the dividend on their few shares will make no significant difference to their standard of living. In general the main benefit to a manager further down the organisation comes from an increase in the size of his department or an increase in the activities of the organisation. Salaries tend to vary with the size of the organisation and not with its profitability. Added to this is the large amount of economic activity provided by non-commercial concerns, where failure to cover the costs is not necessarily fatal to the executive's career; concerns such as those providing fuel, coal, gas, electricity and railway transport, local authority services and all the operations of government-supplied services.

A very high proportion of the spending of money in the community is undertaken by people who are spending other people's money and not their own. The politicians decide on the broad issues and tax the citizens to pay for their schemes; the details are worked out by the civil service. Further expenditure is at local government level. Even the purely business organisation may be heavily reliant on various types of government grant and assistance, or is hopeful of joining in the largesse queue. It is only when we approach the little that is left and we have the housewife using her own money to buy a little more of this and a little less of that, that we come down to the true allocation of scarce resources.

One consequence of this is that organisations may be very efficient if our measure of efficiency is the attainment of some objective. If the object is to give the population what some experts think is good for them; if the object is to prevent change and retain the present way of life; if the object is to expand the size of the organisation and create fresh opportunities within it to enlarge the size and the number of departments; if the object is to diffuse the ownership of the company among a very large number of shareholders living too far away to make it worth their while to attend the company meeting so that they could be a nuisance to the directors; then on these tests many firms could not be faulted for their managerial efficiency. But if a company claims to be in business, and is supposed to be concerned with operating at a profit, and it must be judged by commercial criteria, then far too many companies would fail to pass this efficiency test.

This is not to suggest that managers of other people's money are incompetent in their individual tasks, or that they are robbing the till. Far from it. They may be the most dedicated of men. It is that in the large corporation, as has been pointed out by many observers in recent years, the motives and the pressures that influence the managers are not the same as would influence them in their private lives. There is a great difference between the decisions taken to spend one's own money and the decisions to spend the corporation money. The former is real money and excessive spending can be hurtful. There is a vast difference between before and after tax expenditure. Much of the activity of the people in the large corporation is directed to the corporation as such, and would go on even if the corporation never sold another pennyworth of its product. No. The managers are competent in doing their jobs within the corporation and achieve their objectives; the criticism is that the objectives are wrong and contribute little to the efficiency of the corporation and less to the economy as a whole.

The non-commercial activities may be more efficient in this respect. The civil service has its tradition of public service instead of the profit motive. Its expenditure is governed by rules and this is a curb on private extravagance. But it is one thing for a department which is concerned with government and a service providing that service as its prime objective, and another thing for a commercial firm claiming to provide a public service and trade for the public good, merely because it is unable to trade at a profit.

Management pitfalls

The technology trap Every organisation is producing a product or a service which has to be marketable. It must sell to the general public, even if the 'selling' process consists of levying the taxation which is required to provide a public service. Therefore what is important is the worth of the commodity provided, compared with its cost to the community, either in the form of a price paid directly by the consumer as he buys the article, or in the contribution made by the community to the general taxation fund. The consumer requires clothing either to keep himself warm, or out of prison, or as a status symbol. He requires certain qualities in different articles of clothing, and it is a matter of indifference to him whether the article came from an animal's back, from a plant or from a chemical process. These are technical matters that determine the supply of clothing, and all commodities will have different costs of production and they are in competition with one another. Similarly when the consumer switches on her electricity, it is a matter of indifference to her whether this electricity is produced from a coal- or oil-burning station, a hydro-electric plant, or even a windmill. How the supply is produced will determine the cost and the consumer is interested in the lowest cost supply.

Technology, like research, can be of absorbing interest to those who are involved in it. We must not overlook the advances that have been made by people who have devoted much time and expertise to furthering some idea and to perfecting some process. It is such people who make human advances. But we must remember that all this is a means to an end and if a new method is discovered the old technology may be made obsolete. It is one thing to be interested in technological problems as a hobby after working hours, it is another to play this expensive hobby with other people's money. Many firms have had a reputation for technical excellence but little profit. A man in business on his own may be content with less profit because it is absorbed with the craft of his industry, and this is a sensible decision if such is his own scale of preference. This does not justify the use of other people's money for ends which do not benefit the company.

AEI has always had a reputation for its engineering; Cunard for its passenger ships; Rolls-Royce for its technology. Each company has been taken over in some form or other largely because of a lack of profitability. Such companies are usually dominated by excellent technicians who are uninterested in the business success – but the business failure deprives them of the opportunity to pursue their technology.

Research This is an extension of the technology trap. Companies may spend huge amounts of money in the search for new products or for new methods of production. The only thing certain about expenditure on research and development is that the expenditure is undertaken; costs are incurred. *If* something comes back that is another matter, and can be quite independent of the expenditure. The essential thing is either the idea of where the research is leading, or the ability to recognise the value of some incidental or accidental discovery. Money is no substitute for genius. Like technology, research must recognise that there be some outside profit in the form of human benefit as a result of the research.

But generally the large, old-established corporation or industry has a poor record in this respect. This is why it often takes a hammering from new people with new ideas. There are two aspects of this. Much institutional research is wasted because the research body has everything, money, facilities, staff and support from the top – it has everything except ideas. Many of the results, new inventions, new developments, arise spontaneously or are the result of individuals working on their own, often without money, without magnificent facilities, without staff and opposed by all; this research has nothing in its favour except ideas and results.

Even where such ideas arise in the large corporation there are so many people to be persuaded that the idea is a good one, especially if it is proposed by the wrong people, that it may be difficult to put into practice. Many of the inventions, including commercial or administrative innovations, are initially exploited by their originators founding their own businesses. Later they may sell out to large firms and so capitalise very quickly on their ideas. The inventor becomes a millionaire at a stroke, and the large firm receives a much-needed blood transfusion.

Private research is spread over the variety of popular interests. Institutional research concentrates on the ideas which are fashionable and are officially supported. A large proportion of government-sponsored research is lavished on the aircraft industry; that is, the development of an expensive means of transport that confers no direct benefit on the bulk of the population is assisted. There is a curious 'bottomless pit' about this type of expenditure. There is going to be a loss on this aircraft or engine; but this will give us the expertise to develop an even larger aircraft or engine; this will unfortunately incur a large loss, but it will give us . . . and so on. Or, so the argument runs, the technical improvements will allow us to do research. So technology encourages research and research develops technology and it is possible to live a sheltered life without any reference to the cold world outside, until bankruptcy or a change in government ends the flow of largesse. Advanced modern technology could produce a chromium-plated automated mousetrap, linked to a computer with no expense spared. The business solution could be to buy a pedigree cat. The real entrepreneur is kind to strays.

Even where research produces the answer to a technical problem, there is still the element of judgment or choice in assessing whether the idea is more than an interesting toy, or whether it is commercially sound. 'An interesting toy' was Smeaton's opinion of the Watt engine because of its complications and difficulty of manufacture at that time; he was hardly wrong; it was only the great resources of Boulton which brought eventual success. Is an idea, even if it works, likely to be successful, especially if it flies in the face of current practice? The United Alkali Company turned down the electrolysis process on the advice of their expert chemist. He was paid to give the board advice, he gave it, they took it, and it was wrong. The future of United Alkali was ruined by doing what was the right thing, by setting up a central research laboratory and acting on the advice of the man at the head of it.[5]

Technical failures Nothing that has been written above should be taken to imply that technical matters are unimportant. What is criticised is the pursuit of technology for its own sake, especially with other people's money. But from the invention of the wheel and the lever onwards, technology has of course been of prime importance in raising the level of production – when it works. We are so familiar with the record of modern technical achievements that we are apt to overlook the not inconsiderable technical failures.

With experience there develops a corpus of technical knowledge that can be used over and over again. By now we have developed the technique of building two- or three-storey brick houses and, with luck, even larger structures. It is when the principle is extended to larger buildings, or to using different types of material or different methods of construction, that for all the scientific jargon we are pushing out into the unknown. Parts of medieval cathedrals fell down during building, and even a man of Brassey's skill had a large railway bridge collapse; in spite of all the research and development and management techniques, there are still failures.

In 1965 three of the eight cooling towers at Ferrybridge 'C' power station collapsed. The surviving five had to be strengthened and the failed three rebuilt. The report of the committee of inquiry into the collapse came to the conclusion that the basic problem was that research and experience in cooling tower design had been overtaken by the overriding necessity to build larger towers; it is a waste if this overriding necessity leads to failure. It was dramatically learned from the high rise flats at Ronan Point that damage to a corner of the building caused several floors to fall.

Many reinforced concrete tower blocks have brick facings which are not part of the basic structure. It would appear that the bricks are set in concrete frames instead of steel for cheapness. With maturity the bricks tend to expand and the frames contract under pressure. The result is that the brickwork buckles and, if not treated in time, bricks hurtle to the ground below and some very expensive rebuilding has to be undertaken. The system of box-girder bridge construction has caused a number of disastrous collapses during the building period.

In 1967 a paper read to the Society of the Chemical Industry by Sir Ronald Holroyd gave details of the failure of many new plant installations. New ammonia plants increased the supply from 350 tons to 1,000 tons a day and rendered the old plant obsolete. If all went well there could be a 26 per cent discounted cash flow return on the investment. If it took one year to build production up to 60 per cent of capacity, and two years to 80 per cent, the rate of return would be 16 per cent. However, if there were delays in attaining operating efficiency that restricted them to 30 per cent in the first year, 70 in the second and 90 per cent subsequently, the rate of return fell to 7 per cent. Sir Ronald estimated that delays in building cut the return by 1½ per cent for every six months' hold-up. Some of the faults experienced are faulty design of supports, faulty welding resulting in leaking high-pressure piping, faulty fabrication, improper assembly of compressors; plants have had to be shut down due to failure of a simple piece of equipment.

There was a similar experience in the electricity supply industry. The increase in the size of generators installed meant that they had to be designed anew. It appears that when there is a significant increase in size the previously acquired wisdom is useless and everything has to start from the beginning once more. The result is that well-tried and successful components are abandoned in favour of a new design which may not work. Before the problems of the giant generating set are solved, the industry moves on to the super giant hoping that the previous troubles will not recur.

Computer installations often prove to be failures, although this is more a failure of management induced by the false hope that buying an expensive calculating machine would solve some intractable management problems. This is not a peculiarly British phenomenon, nor does it occur only when the size of the machine is increased. In the USA General Motors and Ford have expanded their range of cars into the 'compacts' – the name given to a European car which would not occupy two parking meters – because of the success of small, imported cars in the American market. In March 1971 Ford had to recall all the 220,000 Pinto models because of a defect that caused fires in the engine compartment; in April 1972 Ford had to announce that it was taking corrective action on practically all its medium-sized car range to alter a faulty axle bearing which could cause the wheels to drop off. General Motors in May 1972 announced that it had to recall 350,000 Vegas. The fault was quite small: a bracket failure interfered with the throttle linkage so that at times when the driver released the throttle the car did not slow down. Yet General Motors had produced millions of cars with throttle pedals that worked properly. It happens over and over again that a motor car which has been designed by experienced engineers, and has had its production broken down into simple components and methods of construction, and has been test run and inspected, will, as soon as it gets into the hands of the man who has paid for it, develop all sorts of troubles. The accumulated wisdom of the past seems to have little effect.

The aircraft industry has an odd technical procedure. An aircraft is produced in the imagination, and then solutions for all the technical problems of power and size and weight and pay loads are worked on. When it was announced that Rolls-Royce had signed a contract to sell an engine to the Lockheed company, it was not realised by those who saw a new dawn that the engine was not built and that the company was budgeting millions of pounds for development costs only, nor that it included an untried product (carbon fibre) which did not come up to expectation. One might be forgiven for believing that here was a great technological break-through in a completely new product, overlooking the fact that there are a number of other manufacturers of similar engines.

One of the few examples of successful technology was the Ferranti work on the 'Bloodhound'. The company contracted to provide electronic equipment for the new missile. The equipment worked; it was produced on time; it was satisfactory in operation. As nothing went wrong a very large profit was made, the 'excess' of which was returned to the government. (Other firms, such as Hawker Siddeley, had lost money on similar fixed-price contracts which in the 1960s were replacing the cost-plus contracts.) The government got what it wanted at the price it had agreed, and instead of the company being congratulated on its efficiency there was a public outcry. Yet if a firm fails to produce the workable article within the time and the price, it can keep going to the government for further grants. Since 1964 this mistake of fulfilling the contract on time at a good profit is not one which many manufacturers have made.

Generally it is unprofitable to pursue research and technology for their own sakes. The costs exceed the benefits. Since the war there has been a concentration on defence, nuclear power and the aircraft industry, which has absorbed a disproportionate amount of money and skilled manpower to the neglect of other opportunities. Part of the waste has been due to an attempt to match American expenditure in these fields, following the theory that if America has it we must have it in order to keep up. But elementary economic theory since Adam Smith explains that all countries do not have to produce the same things, but all can benefit from specialisation and exchange. If the USA can afford to spend more money on certain ideas, such as cancer research, because she is rich enough to afford the losses then it is pointless to try to match this expenditure. It is better to abandon the idea and use the resources for other ideas where less capital expenditure is necessary. The great thing about the Rolls-Royce RB 211 contract in certain political circles was that it 'did down' the American competitors.

At one time it was argued that as Britain had been the pioneer in so many new developments, she had suffered. Britain had borne the cost and the failures and other countries then acquired the textile machinery, the Bessemer converters, the railways and the steamships. So, if Britain suffered by being first, others benefited by being second. But when others take the lead in certain activities, it is now argued that Britain is falling behind and disaster is not far away! It is a waste to try to catch up other countries that have a clear advantage, and to neglect those activities where Britain has a comparative advantage. The inventions and improvements made elsewhere will flow over into Britain in just the same way as British inventions have been applied throughout the world.

Postwar problems

In addition to the technical problems there are general economic problems of a special nature facing the manager. The manager or the entrepreneur always has had to face economic problems, the problem of the market, the problem of making an investment now with the hope of some future return, the problem of producing at a cost below the selling price, and many others. One of the effects of the accumulation of inventions, and the change which these have had on the pattern of life, has been to introduce a special insecurity into business life. Past inventions have brought new methods of satisfying wants which have made old and inefficient methods obsolete; but now further inventions have undermined the earlier ones and have rendered them obsolete in their turn, or if not actually obsolete in physical terms, have made them economically backward.

Although the invention of the railway transformed human transport throughout the world, yet there is hardly a country where railways are not contracting and facing financial difficulties. The later invention of a small power unit has meant that the car and the lorry can now compete. Transport has gone back to its original place, to the roads, and perhaps the 'railway age' may be a peculiar footnote in future economic history. There was a parellel development with sea transport, the application of the steam engine to mechanical improvements. The same small power has been applied to air transport and as a result the large passenger liner is going the way of the long-distance passenger train. If the various inventions had come at the same time the problem would have been which to develop, but once there is a large capital investment in one method of satisfying an economic want, there are strong forces working against the introduction of the new inventions.

In about a hundred years similar techniques have been applied and withdrawn from urban transport. The electric tram was a great improvement in city travel, yet town after town in Britain has scrapped its tramway system. This is an episode which has left little mark on the economy. While the tramway and the railway work essentially on the same principle, there is not the same sentimental impetus to preserve the one as there is for the other. The internal combustion engine has reversed a trend. Mass-production methods using power-driven machinery have concentrated production in larger units and away from the smaller workshop. But the petrol engine decentralises production ('production' here being the creation of a transport utility) back to the small unit. The consumer of transport can even provide his own.

The cinema has had a similar history to that of the tram. A massive entertainment industry grew up, fed by great technical inventions of talking pictures and colour production, but this industry has had to contract in the face of the development of television. Again, a move back to individual consumption, instead of mass enjoyment in a theatre. Even here there are peculiarities which are difficult to foresee. The cinema, and then television, killed the Victorian music hall, but quietly and almost unknown the trend has been reversed in the working-men's clubs in the midlands and the north. This example of self-help would have pleased Samuel Smiles.

In many cases there is a much heavier investment in plant to arrive at the finished product. Textiles such as wool or cotton can still be made by hand on a small scale, and much of the machinery for different processes is still relatively small. A firm may expand by adding small units. The difference between a large and a small firm is not in the type of machines used, but that the larger firm has more of the same type of machine. But in the modern textile industry, using artificial fibres such as nylon, the plant is very large, necessitating a vast capital investment before production can begin. New products are succeeded by newer products. The raised standard of living has increased the variety of goods which are profitable and old goods are dressed up in various ways. One could face the world with porridge, eggs and bacon, toast and marmalade, if the family income were sufficient. The first item is replaced by 'porage' and there is a bewildering choice of breakfast foods. There are heavy promotional expenses in trying to get the new product on to the market.

One attempted solution to this problem is to spread the risk; the multi-product company, dabbling in a variety of goods, is tending to replace the company specialising in one range of goods. But this brings difficulties of a new order. Instead of the single-minded specialisation there is a spread of interests and of knowledge over a variety of activities. There are problems of accounting, costing and control. One cannot just 'play the percentages' and hope that the gains on the swings will overcome the losses on the roundabouts. Decisions still have to be taken, when to expand one line, when to admit the errors and withdraw another line. It is too easy to keep a line going hoping that next year sales will pick up, especially if capital, skill and reputations are committed to that product.

In any case, even where there are successful products, the losses bring down the average return on capital. The generally poor return on capital among the large firms since the war has been a notable feature of the economy. When the swings fail to materialise and there is a higher proportion of roundabouts, disaster is not too far away. There is another purge, another reorganisation, another management reshuffle.

A common method of coping with these economic and business problems is to introduce various techniques and aids to management to replace the flair of the founding entrepreneur – which equally could lead to disaster. But the managers, or their advisers, who form a growth industry in the present century, hope to offset the errors of 'seat of the pants management' or instinctive reaction, by method and organisation.

Management techniques

Managers, rather than entrepreneurs, rely on management techniques as a guide to their work. But too often the rules are confused with the game, and the tools of the trade with the product. Management tools, or 'aids to management', are only aids and not the real thing. A cricket bat is a tool, it is not a late cut executed by a master. The game analogy is an apt one. If Tony Jacklin or Jack Nicklaus won the Open wearing odd socks all the professionals' shops would be stocked with this new aid to concentration and guarantee of success. Why else do successful professionals make a fortune out of endorsing products?

This is not to condemn the proper use of specific techniques in their proper place but to recognise their limitations. Many of them are basically straightforward in principle and most are enlargements on common sense. What is objected to is the superstitious belief that some new and fashionable idea is going to solve all management problems. The fields of management are scarred by deep ruts cut by the passage of the fashionable band-wagons.

Many of these techniques are eventually regarded as failures by the managers. This is so because when a new fashion appears over the horizon the old one falls from favour. Like the Athenians, managers run after strange gods, and these gods are known by their initials, such as PERT, MBO, DCF and other peculiar combinations. Some very good servants become bad masters and some walking-sticks end up as necessary crutches.

The beginning of it goes back to the alleged scientific management associated with the work of F. W. Taylor and developed by his disciples. (The master is always referred to by them with the full name of Frederick Winslow Taylor.) One of Taylor's techniques was to study the work in the engineering factory where he was a manager. He suspected that the workers were not working hard enough, a suspicion still to be found in modern managers. But to determine what was 'enough' meant that the work had to be measured and timed. The invention of the stop watch was of great assistance here. He therefore studied how the work was done. The job was broken down into its elementary parts. All unnecessary movements were eliminated. The best method was discovered. The workmen were trained in this 'best method'. It was all timed and a time allowance given for each job.

It is not known whether Taylor had read economics, but all economists are familiar with Adam Smith's pin factory where the principle of division of labour (or specialisation) was practised, where one man draws out the wire, another cuts it into lengths, another sharpens the pin – and it is even a trade in itself to put the pins into the packet. The principle of course was not new even in Adam Smith's day, it goes back at least to Xenophon, but Taylor did systematise it from the management point of view. It must be pointed out that in the USA of that time, the late nineteenth century, conditions were rather special. Unlike Britain, where there was the tradition of apprenticeship so that the individual workman could be expected to contribute some skill to the work, many of the employees in the USA were immigrants without an industrial background. Many could not speak English. The work had to be organised so that an immigrant in urgent need of work could be taken to a machine, shown by signs what buttons to push or levers to pull, and left to get on with it.

Taylor was also concerned with other important aspects such as the need for the proper tools to be supplied to the workmen by the establishment of a toolroom; the standardisation of materials, proper working conditions, etc. He did succeed in raising the output of American engineering shops. But the methods required costly and elaborate organisational systems to control the work of the operators, so that part of the savings of cruder manpower was absorbed by the expense of organisation. There is also the importance of the personal qualities and drive of the founders of the cult in achieving successes. The great American expansion of industry did not depend on scientific management, and the great captains such as Carnegie and Ford built up their industries without having heard of the idea. Taylor was a works manager, later a consultant and not an entrepreneur, which probably explains why he is more of a hero to the professional manager than he is to the businessman.

One detrimental, and mistaken, idea which arose from the dividing of a process into distinct functions was that people should spend their lives in dull, repetitive tasks. Another was in the separation of planning and doing. Somebody, or a number of people, tell the operator exactly how he is to do his job as though he were a tool only, and a mindless moron. 'Scientific' management is most unscientific when it fails in labour management. It cannot even buy contentment and industrial peace with high earnings. Temporary strikes are a necessary safety valve in such conditions of work.

Scientific management acquired such a bad reputation on the labour side in the USA and Britain that it gave way to work study. The reader will find that most textbooks on the subject are divided into two sections, time study and motion study, so the same broad ideas are being presented differently. If it changes to organisation and methods the blow is softened. But there is still too much emphasis on the old-fashioned time and motion study, with its stop watches, piece rates, arguments with shop stewards; British Leyland and other sections of the motor industry are laboriously, and expensively, trying to get away from this idea.

Another example of applying specific techniques to management problems is the recording of work to be done, and showing in an easily observable form the progress of this work through the organisation. The method varies with the type of work. It is at its simplest where there is a single product or service being produced or operated, such as a cotton mill, or a bakery, or the operation of a complicated railway network in a country like Britain. In flow-assembly plants, such as in the manufacture of radios or motor cars, the trick is setting up the production line and arranging for the flow of components at the right time and place. But after that the routine checking is relatively simple. It is much more difficult to organise manufacture in a jobbing factory or where there is a great variety of work. Variations of the Gantt chart, where lines represent time, are used to give a visual and pictorial aid to progressing the work.

In the early 1960s there were two prospects of salvation from management problems: Programme Evaluation and Review Technique, PERT, and Critical Path Analysis, CPA. In addition to the preparation of the whole programme a schedule is made out for the various parts of the programme. PERT requires regular checking to ensure that each part of the programme is advancing as planned, and CPA requires a chart which shows the time of the operations and how they all fit together; and it shows which operations are critical to the time span and which are not. In its simplest form, say in house building, electricians and plasterers cannot begin work until the foundations are laid and the shell completed, fittings have to be ordered a number of weeks before they are required and so on. It concentrates the mind on the fact that before the roof is finished orders for sinks and baths have to go in although they are not yet wanted. Again this should be obvious but the introduction of some method means that routine decisions can be anticipated so as to avoid a panic search for materials at the last minute.

As always, there is a certain disillusion with overfond hopes of management ease. Some companies have thrown out the new systems and reverted to bar charts and other older methods. What must be made quite clear is that a network analysis, or any other device, only shows what ought to happen. It does not make it happen. Completion may be held up by the failure to receive some minor component and a job which is scheduled to take ten days may take twenty, putting the whole programme out. In view of the common failure to complete a job on time or to eliminate 'teething troubles' what is needed is less review techniques and more performance.

The really new management model, corresponding to the gas turbine car, is MBO, Management by Objectives. The basic idea is that managers are set various objectives (they may contribute to the setting of the targets) and at the end of a set period the manager is judged by the degree to which he has attained his objective. As was pointed out at the beginning of this chapter, the simplest objective is survival followed by survival at a profit, but it is difficult to relate this concept to individual actions which may have no bearing on the profitability of the enterprise. The trick surely is seeing that the right objectives are set and that they are relevant to the success of the whole. For example, the personnel department is instructed to recruit a hundred university graduates in assorted disciplines as part of the management development scheme. One hundred are recruited. The objective has been achieved. Promotion prospects in the department look rosy. But how many of these recruits will still be with the firm in two years' time? How many will still be there in five years, filling in some middle management position? How many will be valuable to the company at the top after twenty years? The company may be disappointed with the whole approach and change its policy.

As with other models there are specifications and instructions couched in special languages, job descriptions, key analysis areas, effectiveness areas, managerial objective meeting, the team objective meeting. The outsider who is not privy to the jargon of the club membership is amazed, both that such common sense and ancient ideas are elevated into a new philosophy when it is as old as Aristotle, and that it should be necessary to tell managers this at all. MBO, like so many other techniques, is such a BGO (Blinding Glimpse of the Obvious) that it is disquieting to find that it should be deemed necessary.

Many firms before the war introduced budgetary control, which started with the financial objectives and then went on to sales and production and manpower objectives (such as the recruiting of a hundred graduates?) necessary to achieve this result. The principle was common in department stores, on a half-yearly basis. All of these systems are laudable attempts at planning the future, setting down the necessary data, and checking on the results.

One objective is the financial return to be obtained from an investment of capital. There are various means of doing this, and the most fashionable is DCF. This should please the professional economist, because all that it is, is an old economic truth which economists have had difficulty in getting over, but which is now obtaining some acceptance provided that it is couched in a new language. The basic principle is that a pound today is worth more than a pound tomorrow, or that time is money and interest is the price of time. So, in evaluating the profitability of an investment some allowance must be made for the time which elapses before the results flow in. The future benefit is discounted by the rate of interest, hence the discounted cash flow. Another way of looking at it is, that a flow of future benefits can be discounted to give the present value. For example the purchase price of an annuity is the present value of a flow of future income.

Once again, it is the case that overenthusiastic discoverers of the rate of interest have taken this to be an answer to management problems. Calculating the expected cash flow from an investment over the next ten years, while better than a blind dash into the future, does not of course ensure that the results will be achieved; there are risks and uncertainties in all future planning and the best-prepared schemes may go wrong. It is to be supposed that the ill-prepared schemes will fare even worse.

Selection procedures have not succeeded in producing the right people to fill vacancies. There is a high failure rate. The real difficulty here is in trying to assess a young man's performance in several years' time. One recruitment officer, with becoming modesty, stated that he dreaded rejecting someone who would turn up later as the managing director of ICI. He may be comforted by the thought that the engagement of the twelve apostles had a 25 per cent failure rate, with a very serious deficiency in one of the trainees, in spite of divine guidance.

Accounting has not succeeded in being the aid to management that was expected. Much of it is the routine recording of the daily transactions, the results of which are filed away. Yet, as Dr Drucker points out (*Managing for Results*) the accounts contain a mass of information, which if properly analysed would be invaluable in improving the profitability of a business. To take two simple examples. A firm dealing with a large number of customers may find that a comparatively small number of them are responsible for the bulk of the orders; a large number of customers place such small orders that they do not merit the postage and bookkeeping costs in servicing their accounts. A multi-product firm may be producing short runs of expensive, poor-selling products which are not discontinued because Cousin Charlie is interested in them. This is one reason why when someone with an analytical approach takes over, the slack can be taken up and some dramatic improvements in profits can result.

Accounting has its fairly simple systems of recording costs. There is more to costing than sticking 100 per cent on labour costs. 'The cost of an article' can have several different meanings according to circumstances, and these different circumstances affect management decisions. In the interwar years there was some notable development of marginal cost theories applied to the problems of the firm. Some of this seeped through to accounting in discussions of marginal costing, but the principle does not appear to have gained general acceptance. Accounting keeps records in money which is assumed to have a permanent and unchanging value and very little notice has been taken of the depreciation in the value of money and the effects of inflation in falsifying accounts. When economists complain to the Inland Revenue that firms are overtaxed because conventional accounts exaggerate the real profit, the latter can claim the support of the conventional methods used by the accounting profession. (An interesting sidelight here is that the 'profession' is deemed to be accountants and auditors in private practice – the medieval master-man – and the accountant in industry is a much lesser being.)

In the field of human relations there is a theory X and a theory Y. It seems that some manage their businesses autocratically and others democratically, although why this great truth should be X and Y is not clear.

Two other management ideas are new, or fashionable. One is group technology, described as 'an exciting new technique for managing production'. In the layout of the conventional workshop for batch engineering production, the work proceeds from one set of machines in one department to another. Each section is specialised on a particular range of techniques, and the work passes from one to the other, and back again, according to the function. An army of progress chasers follows the work through the factory. In fact this is the organisation that has developed from the ideas of 'scientific management'. The basic idea of group technology is to organise the men into small groups, where they will be responsible for producing a range of similar parts. All the required tools will be in the group. The parts enter the cells raw and emerge as complete articles. What is really happening is that the work of a large workshop is being broken down into smaller units. It might be said that this system is part of the general thesis that the only way to manage a large undertaking is to treat it as a series of small undertakings, and thus destroy or weaken the alleged advantages of the large unit.

The principle has certainly been operated before the war in office work, without it acquiring any special nomenclature. Instead of one office handling the orders, another dealing with dispatch, another with ledgers and so on, sales have been divided into areas and a small group of about sixteen has handled all the work, dealing with salesmen, processing the invoices, rendering the accounts, and other self-contained cells have dealt with other areas. The main advantage claimed for this, as for group technology, is the greater interest of the job, where there is more variety of work and employees can see more clearly their contribution to the finished product.

The other new development is 'venture management'. The object is to separate the organisation man from the adventurer in the large corporation. By various means, such as setting up separate companies or groups semi-independently, the managers operate as if they were independent entrepreneurs. One of the main disadvantages of all business, and large-scale business in particular, is that so much time is necessarily taken up with the day-to-day operations that little time and energy can be put into new products and new ideas. Where so much emphasis has been placed on the conformity of the organisation man, the companies find difficulty in obtaining the constructive nonconformist. Hence venture management.

One technique which is now losing favour is that of 'putting it on the computer'. The touching faith in the ability of a computer to solve management problems is fading with experience. A computer is a machine that adds one to one, or it accepts or rejects one, but it does these tasks very quickly. Where there is a large volume of routine clerical work, such as handling thousands of wage payments a week, or dealing with a large number of customers, a properly installed computer system will save enough labour to justify its high capital cost. It is an extension of the principle of applying machinery to office work. It can also do very complicated calculations very quickly.

Solving the mathematical calculations is, however, not solving the underlying technical problems. No matter how carefully stresses are calculated, bridges and tower blocks fall down, wings fall off aeroplanes and expected performance is not achieved. Computers have not made test pilots redundant. The other limitation is that the answer produced by the computer depends on the data that is fed in. This is not understood by those unaccustomed to mathematical or economic analysis. In order to reduce the problem to a formula that can be represented in arithmetical terms it is necessary to make certain assumptions, for example, the rate of expansion of the market will be 5 per cent. Of course a whole series of different calculations can be run off on the assumption that the market will expand by 4 per cent, 8 per cent and so on, or on the assumption that there is going to be no strike in the industry, that there is going to be a four-day strike in the sixth week of production, and thousands of other possible combinations. The computer can say 'yes' or 'no' and it does it very quickly, but it cannot explain which of the many assumptions is likely to prove correct. Here human managerial judgment has to be exercised. It has been said that a computer can baldly say 'no' but a lady can say 'no' in a tone of voice which leaves some hope. A computer has no tone of voice.

The really important business decisions are those where current expenditure takes place with a view to a future benefit. Neither can be foreseen with any accuracy. The computer has not succeeded where the fortune teller, the tea leaf contemplator, the priest slaughtering some innocent fowls, have all failed. Reliance on 'our computer told us to' may prove as catastrophic as faith in the Delphic oracle. When Croesus asked it what would happen if he attacked Persia it said that 'a great empire' would fall, but omitted to make it clear that it was his own empire that would fall; and when it told the Athenians to rely on their 'wooden walls' those who took the advice and retreated behind the wooden wall of the Acropolis were overrun by the Persians. Salvation came from the wooden walls of the ships at Salamis.

According to one of the leading management consultants in Britain, Urwick Orr, 80 per cent of computer installations in the USA and Europe fail to show an economic return on investment, 40 per cent of computer users show a worsening in performance in the areas of their business where computers are applied, and many others level the same criticism (*Financial Times*, 5 March 1971).

Professional managers have the advantage of using their professional associations and other bodies to assist them in their tasks. Yet who will guard the guardians? These bodies may be subject to the same ills as the businesses that are advised or directed by their own members. In May 1971 the Council of the Institute of Chartered Accountants was severely criticised by the members at the annual general meeting. In the previous year £45,000 had been lost but that year the institute achieved a £369,000 deficit. The reasons for this deficit are the familiar ones that professional managers could charge against any incompetent business. Of course it had a computer, estimated to cost £25,000 but to date the cost was £127,000. Of course it had a new tower office block, and had failed to let off two floors and so had to forgo £60,000 expected revenue. The budgetary system was inadequate. And of course consultants had been called in and 'the accounts department is now in pretty good order'.

The consultants may find that they are faced with the same commercial problems as their clients. The Production Engineering Research Association (PERA) set up a purpose-built conference centre in Melton Mowbray in 1962. In 1972, owing to the decline in the market for management conferences and the mounting losses, the conference centre was closed. This did not affect the education and training services which were to be continued.

The building and construction industry is always being castigated by its critics, for its lack of management expertise and for its failure to run training programmes. It had to be forced to train its employees to make the industry more efficient. In 1966 the Construction Industry Training Board was set up. As with similar boards, all firms in the industry had to pay a compulsory levy, whether they required the board's services or not. Grants were made to firms that introduced approved training schemes or courses, irrespective of the size of the contribution to the fund. The economist will quickly see that some schemes could be introduced, not because of a sudden conversion to management education but to pick up some of the cash freely available. But many people in the industry, especially among the small firms, tended to be suspicious of outside direction; the entrepreneurial attitude is not quite dead.

The result was that as money flowed in under compulsion, it did not flow out. Cash accumulated to between £2–4 million by 1969. So the board worked very hard to inform the builders that this money was available, freely, to encourage 'training'. Eventually the penny dropped – and so did the millions of surplus, as builders accepted the invitation to 'get your whack'. Soon the surplus became an overdraft of over £6 million. In January 1970 Cooper Brothers, the accountants, were called in by the board to find out the cause of the trouble. Besides criticising the system where the board's income was fixed by the levy but its expenditure was open-ended in that firms did the training and then put in the claim, the auditors took the board to task for its lack of financial planning and budgetary control. The board's chief executive, responsible for the day-to-day running since 1965 and also a well-known management consultant and author of one of the standard text-books on management, resigned in 1970 (*Sunday Times*, 9 August 1970).

The British Institute of Management, which was set up after the war to improve British management, is not immune from market forces. In its annual report for the year ended 31 March 1972 (but published on 12 September 1972, hardly a good example of accounting speed), a loss of £109,000 was disclosed. Two contributing factors were that it had held back planned increases in course fees as part of the price restraint policy, and that there had been a reduction of £33,000 in the government grant. It had been supported by grants from its inception but the government was coming round to the view that the institute ought to be self-supporting. But the main cause of the loss had been a heavy fall in the management course market. Many arranged courses had to be cancelled and the members attending were almost halved.

In its task of improving management, and supporting the principle of 'professional management', it followed various avenues. There was the individual member as in other professional associations, admitted by examination, although the captains of industry were not subject to this indignity. A member's main association was through his local branch rather than the head office. There were the corporate subscribers who had access to services not available to ordinary members. Added to this there was the provision of courses and conferences on a variety of subjects, the mixture depending on the supply of new fashionable ideas, such as MBO. Many of the ordinary members felt that the BIM devoted attention to this type of work to the neglect of the private members' interests. It was the failure in the course market which brought the loss and ate up the institute's reserves. It also caused a considerable decline in staff, adding to the BIM's reputation for periodic purges. One of the reforms was to make a start in putting in a budgetary control system. How many courses on budgetary control and similar topics must the BIM have put before the public?

A feature of postwar industry has been the use of consultants, one of the truly growth industries of the period. Professor Parkinson asked why should a board of directors, presumably chosen for their competence and advised by able and experienced executives, have to call in outsiders to tell them how to run their business? Of course, the idea that the king consults with the council or the elders of the tribe before undertaking action goes back to antiquity, but the directors are themselves the elders of the tribe, and it will be remembered from an earlier chapter that they contribute 'wise counsel'.

In general, consultants may not be the elders. In some professions the consultant is a senior man who is consulted precisely because of his greater knowledge and experience. In management consultancy many of the practitioners are young and less experienced; in fact a young man can be advised to further his own career by spending a few years in management consultancy before settling down into line management. He can learn the trade by practising it on others, which is reminiscent of the practice of sending the sons of the nobility on the grand tour. Their wild oats could be sown in some foreign field.

One justification is that knowledge acquired by an assignment in one firm can be applied to others. Like the bees they transfer the pollen from flower to flower, and although they assist in the process they must not suffer from the delusion that they are taking part in the process of creation. Bessemer in his *Autobiography* related how he visited the works of a friend and immediately pointed out an improvement that had not been apparent to the man who had been in that business for many years. This is the benefit of the outside view. But we are not all Bessemers. Nor did he set up as a consultant!

There is still a large element of the early time and motion study work in use today. Much is made of the new techniques discussed above. Each new fad can shine like a blinding light and, like Saul on the Damascus road, there is the strong incentive to spread the message to the Gentiles. When a firm like McKinsey gets away from the workshop-floor type of investigation, it collars the market.

However, the main field of activity is where there is a 'one-off' job or where something happens infrequently so that it is not to be expected that the directors will have some previous experience to guide them. One clear example is an issue of capital. An elementary bookkeeping textbook will give the accounts and the entries for a share issue. Few accountants in industry will have had actual experience of the organisation of an issue. To the specialist merchant banker it is a routine operation. No respectable firm today can be without its own merchant banker, to assist it in making a bid for a rival, or to defend it against the predator, or to grant a watching brief in case it is drawn into the struggle. The 'one-off' jobs occur where a firm is making a fundamental change in its methods of production, or trying to break into a new type of market, or where the family-type business has outgrown individual management and has to change its methods and organisation or face a decline.

While we cannot judge the efficiency of management in detail we can look at the picture as a whole. Here there are two points of view. One is the decline theory; the decay of the manor; the decay of the yeomanry; the loss of leadership; the falling behind in the face of competitors; the increasing wealth of other countries; the loss of empire, and a long tale of woe that passes for the economic history of this country. On the other hand there is the clear indication that there has been an absolute increase in production, a greater volume of real wealth, a reduction in poverty, and an attack on the hard core of unemployment that was the main scourge of the interwar years; there is the clear evidence of better food and clothing and increased leisure time for the bulk of the working population. There are pockets of poverty, affecting especially the old, where the improvement has not been equal and all-embracing, but these are outside the scope of this book. In spite of the critics' view of a shifty and workshy labour force, an incompetent management and a guilty-men set of politicians, the standard of living does rise.

Could it be better? To be scientific we must have a measure of efficiency and this is lacking, except in the small-scale competitive industry where there is a rough justice measure. Management has not solved the problem of costing the operations in different processes and in multi-product operations. It has not solved the accounting problems of valuations of stock and work-in-progress, where variations in these figures can convert profits into losses and vice-versa. It may be that there is no absolute solution to this problem and any treatment is a compromise of conflicting ideas – that is, the problem has not been solved because there is no solution. This still affects the main argument that it is difficult to judge the efficiency of management.

One obvious way of improving the industrial efficiency of the country is to expand the efficient industries at the expense of the inefficient. If resources are used where they give the greatest return the general level will be raised. Where people are spending their own money they will soon decide to cut out those activities where the cost exceeds the benefit. If they do not, they will suffer the consequences. Their own pockets will be hurt. A very large part of the spending in this country is directed by people and administered by other people who have no direct financial responsibility for their actions. If the failures are too spectacular there may be some loss of career prospects, but not the financial ruin that overtakes the entrepreneur.[6]

In a country of over fifty million people, with an inherited capital, a skilled labour force and an industrial tradition, it is impossible to know what activities are efficient or are inefficient. To feed this population requires large agricultural subsidies, to house them requires vast government subsidies and encouragement. Such a market for goods and services should be a gift for an able entrepreneur, yet the government has to make grants, to devise investment incentives, and to induce businessmen to lay out capital. It increases the handout if the investment is made in an area chosen by the government. Millions of pounds of taxpayers' money are lost in moving the people from one place to another in their daily work; yet the same people spend millions of pounds of their own money in taxation to provide themselves with private transport to take their families to the seaside. Money is poured into prestige activities at the expense of raising the standard of living of the poorer sections of the population.

Executives, on tax deductible expense accounts, fly on subsidised aircraft, powered by subsidised engines between loss-making airports; commuters travel from their subsidised council houses or tax-assisted mortgage residences on subsidised trains to a place of work bolstered up by grants and other subventions. The working classes have to be taxed to pay the subsidies on housing to bring the houses up to the standard that the middle classes believe the workers ought to want. The workers are beginning to rumble the whole process. They now talk of their 'take home' pay, *after* tax. The money collected from them to be used to provide what the managers want does not count. Only the net amount, what they can spend themselves, is real money.

Another failure of the manager in industry is in labour relations. The self-made man who has risen from the ranks is not always a good employer, but on the whole the most successful were not as bad as many of them have been painted. They did understand the class from which they had come and they could enjoy a certain amount of respect. The present-day manager comes from a different background, different both from that of the owner-manager and of the workers. In large firms and in nationalised industries negotiations are between the workers (one set of employees) and the managers (another set of employees). In fact the managers, acting on behalf of the firm, may be in a more precarious position than the workers. Many present-day managers are treated by their firms in the same way as the early factory owners were alleged to have treated their hands; or in the way that the old nobility treated the peasants before the revolution, but the peasants are no longer submissive or content with their old station in life. The French Revolution liberated the managerial class from the yoke of the aristocracy. Its effects are still being worked out further down the social scale. Management has not solved the problem of industrial relations and proper leadership. Like the Caliph who was unable to administer justice in the distant parts of his empire, modern management builds up businesses that it is unable to control.

However, there are some faint signs of improvement. There are rumours of disenchantment with the vast corporation; there is dissatisfaction with sets of accounts presenting 'a true and fair view' of the company's affairs which conceal the operations of the company in consolidated accounts; it is still too easy for the plausible rogue to despoil the public, but it is easier still for the self-opinionated and incompetent to bring ruin and loss on others. There are even signs that a way must be found for the competition of newcomers to infuse the old, stodgy, managed firms with new energy. But the real test of efficiency is to ask the question 'Would you do it if it were your own money?'

Notes

1 A. C. Pigou, *The Economics of Welfare,* Macmillan, 1920.

2 The costs of different plants *can* be compared, yet many multi-plant firms still retain high-cost factories within their group, and they continue to be high-cost producers.

3 Some years ago I visited a large number of firms to study their problems and organisation. In one, which was in a contracting and loss-making industry, the production control system was the same as that in a nearby firm in an expanding industry. The staff did the same work.

4 While learning, errors were inevitable. Some of the sagas of 'the day I got converted' have been told with loving relish and may be passed down into English folklore.

5 W. J. Reader, *Imperial Chemical Industries; A History*, vol. 1, Oxford University Press, 1970, p. 119.

6 The career can end, perhaps temporarily, with a large payment of compensation for loss of office, where the executive director has had the foresight to write in a good service contract.

A guide to further reading

The student of the development of business organisation and management is confronted with a wide choice of books and articles. Some are books to commemorate an anniversary in the company's history, or the great deeds of its colourful founder, or perhaps his misdeeds. Even these contribute something to knowledge. At the other end are scholarly works of research and analysis, either in book form or tucked away in articles in learned journals such as the *Economic History Review*. The *Dictionary of National Biography* is often very useful. Nearer our own day there are fewer biographies and autobiographies of business leaders. These tend to skim over some of the more interesting details. They do not say the harsh things about their rivals, and their friends too, that are to be found in political memoirs.

'Happy is the firm that has no history' and a great deal of the knowledge of business management in practice blossoms when things go wrong. There are inquiries, commissions and auditors' reports which show the organisations behind the façade. Business papers and the business sections of the quality press are a source of up-to-date information. The inexperienced student must remember that good journalism is not necessarily economic science. The student will have to make his own interpretations.

I have omitted books on general management theory and books on particular techniques of management. On the whole these will be of interest only to those who are concerned with, and have to master, these techniques, i.e. costing, management accounting, labour management, control systems, etc. A list would be too long and liable to change with fashion. In any case here we are more concerned with the body than the limbs, the whole rather than the part.

Early period

LAMOND, ELIZABETH, *Walter of Henley's Husbandry and Other*

Works, 1890. This contains a collection of books on estate management and gives the duties of the many officials.

MOORMAN, J. R. H., *Church Life in England in the Thirteenth Century*, Cambridge University Press, 1945. There are good descriptions of the organisation of the bishopric as a form of church management, and an entertaining account of monasteries.

Early industry

ADDIS, JOHN P., *The Crawshay Dynasty*, University of Wales Press, 1957.

BESSEMER, SIR HENRY, *An Autobiography*, Engineering, 1905.

DEFOE, DANIEL, *The Complete English Tradesman*, 1st ed. 1725–7. Besides being a source book of the organisation of large-scale trading, it contains much sound advice which is ignored today.

ERICKSON, CHARLOTTE, *British Industrialists. Steel and Hosiery, 1850–1950*, Oxford University Press, 1959.

FLINN, M. W., *The Law Book of the Crowley Ironworks*, Surtees Society, 1957.

FLINN, M. W., *Men of Iron*, Edinburgh University Press, 1962. These two books show how Crowley's remarkable business was operated.

HELPS, ARTHUR, *The Life and Labours of Mr Brassey, 1805–70*, Evelyn, Adams & Mackay, 1969. Brassey was one of the great contractors who built railways all over the world.

KINGSFORD, P. W., *F. W. Lanchester*, Edward Arnold, 1960.

LAMBERT, R. S., *The Railway King*, Allen & Unwin, 1934.

LAMBERT, R. S., *The Universal Provider*, Harrap, 1938. These two books are good accounts of the business methods of George Hudson and William Whiteley.

MCKENDRICK, N., 'Josiah Wedgwood, an eighteenth-century entrepreneur in salesmanship and marketing techniques', *Economic History Review*, vol. xii, no. 3, April 1960. This supplements the standard biographies with a detailed analysis of his marketing methods.

MUSSON, A. E., 'James Nasmyth and the early growth of mechanical engineering', *Economic History Review*, vol. x, 1957–8. This is very good on workshop organisation.

RAISTRICK, ARTHUR, *Dynasty of Ironfounders*, Longman, 1953. The classic account of the Darby business.

ROLL, ERIC, *An Early Experiment in Industrial Organisation,* Longman, 1930. Another classic, on the organisation of Boulton and Watt. There are also good biographies.

SMILES, SAMUEL, *Industrial Biography,* 1884. It is fashionable to deride him but he cannot be ignored for this account of the engineering firms, and for his *Lives of the Engineers* and *Self Help.*

The moderns

ANDREWS, P. W. S. and BRUNNER, ELIZABETH, *The Life of Lord Nuffield,* Blackwell, 1955.

BANNOCK, GRAHAM, *The Juggernauts. The Age of the Big Corporation,* Weidenfeld & Nicolson, 1971.

DRUCKER, PETER, *Managing for Results,* Pan, 1967.

EDWARDS, R. S. and TOWNSEND, H., *Business Enterprise. Its Growth and Organisation,* Macmillan, 1965.

JAY, A., *Management and Machiavelli,* Hodder & Stoughton, 1967.

JERVIS, F. R., *The Economics of Mergers,* Routledge & Kegan Paul, 1971.

JONES, R. and MARRIOTT, O., *Anatomy of a Merger,* Cape, 1970. The background history of the companies that ended up in GEC.

LATHAM, SIR JOSEPH, *Take-Over. The Facts and Myths of the GEC/AEI Battle,* Iliffe Books, 1969. Another view of the above.

ROWLEY, C. K., *The British Monopolies Commission,* Allen & Unwin, 1966. There is a lot of information about industries, culled from the Commission's Reports.

THOMAS, SIR MILES, *Out on a Wing,* Michael Joseph, 1964. Another view of Morris Motors management.

TURNER, GRAHAM, *Business in Britain,* Eyre & Spottiswoode, 1969. He has the journalist's flair for collecting a mass of interesting information.

WILSON, CHARLES, *The History of Unilever,* vol. 1, Cassell, 1954. Essential reading. Vols. 2 and 3 deal with later aspects of the business.

WOOLTON, EARL, *Memoirs of Earl Woolton,* Cassell, 1959.

Index